Children No More

How We Lost a Generation

by *Brenda Scott*

Huntington House Publishers

Huntington House Publishers
P.O. Box 53788
Lafayette, Louisiana 70505

Library of Congress Card Catalog Number
94-79917
ISBN 1-56384-083-9

Printed in the U.S.A.

Chapter Design by Jaynell Snyder Trosclair

This book is dedicated to
Sean, Brett and Stephanie.

Always delight yourselves in God
and He will give you your heart's desire.
You are the hope of the future.
I love you.
Mom

Contents

Introduction

Tiny babies line the neonatal nursery, hooked to endless monitors. These pathetic little bundles, crying out in pain, are crack addicts.

A fourteen-year-old boy glances over his shoulder as a car careens around the corner and charges toward him. He begins to run, but it's too late. Just a few feet from home, the youth crumbles under a hail of bullets.

She walks the busy street in hot pants, shivering in the cold, looking for a customer. Her eyes are much older than her thirteen-year-old face. A car pulls over to the curb, the door opens, and she gets in.

These are the changing faces of childhood in America.

Children No More: How We Lost a Generation examines the radically different world our young people encounter, the forces behind the change, and strategies for reclaiming lost ground.

1

Fall from Grace

The deterioration of a government begins almost always by the decay of its principles.
—Montesquieu in *De l'Esprit*

In 1988, Barbara Walters hosted a television special called "America's Kids: Why They Flunk." Her surveys pointed to a deplorable lack of knowledge among the high school students. For example, most of those interviewed were not even able to locate the United States on a map and thought the Holocaust was a "Jewish holiday." But, the problem, she claimed, ran deeper. " 'Today's high school seniors live in a world of misplaced values,' she said. They have no sense of discipline. No goals. They care only for themselves. In short, they are 'becoming a generation of undisciplined cultural barbarians.' "[1]

She was right.

Anything Goes

We are living in a society that no longer accepts an absolute standard of right and wrong; where Judeo-Christian ethics have been replaced with the

9

moral relativism of secular humanism. "Truth has become a matter of taste; morality a matter of preference."[2]

The message today's young people receive is that virtue is not definable—or even desirable. In a survey of 3,795 kids (ages eleven–eighteen), 57 percent said that no objective standard of truth exists, and 85 percent believed that whether or not an action was right or wrong depended solely upon the circumstances. Almost half of the teens agreed with the statement "Everything in life is negotiable."[3] The survey also revealed that those who denied the existence of absolutes were

- 48 percent more likely to cheat on an exam
- two times more likely to watch a pornographic film
- two times more likely to steal
- three times more likely to use illegal drugs
- six times more likely to attempt suicide
- two times more likely to be lacking purpose
- two times more likely to be resentful[4]

Children need the security of boundaries and a solid value-basis for judgment, yet we treat them as if they were born adults. We present them with a smorgasbord of choices and then leave them defenseless and unequipped to make reasoned decisions. Yet, this "freedom" from the bondage of absolute values has not brought the utopia promised by humanists. The kids interviewed in the study above responded that they were confused (55 percent), stressed out (50 percent), and always tired (46 percent).

It has also created a generation of lost children, unprepared to live in a society governed by laws;

incapable of respecting the rights of others; and unable to distinguish between acceptable and unacceptable behavior. In a study conducted with seventeen hundred middle school students in Rhode Island, 65 percent of the boys and 47 percent of the girls agreed that it was okay to force sex on a person after six months of dating. One-fourth of the boys and one-sixth of the girls also agreed that it was okay to force sex on a date if you have spent money on the person.[5] In a similar survey, 20 percent of the girls and 40 percent of the boys responded that it was okay to force sex upon a girl if she had been drinking. It's no wonder date rape is on the rise on college campuses. If there are no absolutes, then anything goes.

Finding Our Roots

Alexis de Tocqueville, the famous nineteenth-century French historian who authored *Democracy in America* observed, "America is great because she is good. If she ever ceases to be good she will cease to be great." As a political philosopher, Tocqueville was fascinated with the form of government that had been created in America. He was also curious regarding the reasons the American Revolution succeeded in producing a free, law-abiding nation based upon principles of liberty, justice, and equality, while the French Revolution had degenerated into a horrendous bloodbath and ultimately ended in a dictatorship.

The difference, he decided, was the religious faith of America's founders which contrasted sharply with the antagonistic atheism of the French revolutionaries.

The religious atmosphere of the country was the first thing that struck me upon my arrival in the United States. The longer I stayed in the country, the more conscious I became of the important political consequences resulting from the novel situation. . . .

I see the destiny of America embodied in the first Puritan who landed on those shores, just as the whole human race was represented by the first man. . . . Their ancestors gave them the love of equality and of freedom; but God himself gave them the means of remaining equal and free. . . .

There is no country in the world where the Christian religion retains a greater influence over the souls of men than in America; and there can be no greater proof of its utility and of its conformity to human nature than that its influence is powerfully felt over the most enlightened and free nation of the earth.[6]

State and Religion

Tocqueville saw the First Amendment in action as it was intended. No man was forced to go to church or to any particular sect; yet most men professed a strong faith in God, and religion was a central part in everyday life. Each faith, though it may differ in catechism and engage in spirited debate, respected the rights and freedoms of the others. No single denomination controlled the government, yet elected officials were also deeply involved in their faith and recognized the need for Christian principles. And, *no one* saw this as a violation of the First Amendment. No one believed that Christians should be exempted from running for public office or engaging in political debate. In fact, the opposite was true.

The Americans combine the notions of Christianity and of liberty so intimately in their minds that it is impossible to make them conceive the one without the other; and with them this conviction does not spring from that barren, traditionary faith which seems to vegetate rather than to live in the soul. . . .

I do not know whether all Americans have a sincere faith in their religion—for who can search the human heart?—but I am certain that they hold it to be indispensable to the maintenance of republican institutions. This opinion is not peculiar to a class of citizens or to a party, but it belongs to the whole nation. . . .

Despotism may govern without faith, but liberty cannot.[7]

Changing Tides

America's Founding Fathers recognized the absolute necessity of divine guidance in leading a free people. As the power of government lessened, the need for self-government increased. This tenuous relationship was acknowledged by Benjamin Franklin. After leaving the Constitutional Convention, he was asked, "Sir, what form of government have you given us?" He replied, "A republic, Madame, if you can keep it."

The problem with society, however, is human nature. Within each person is a need for boundaries and a natural rebellion against them. And, while our forefathers recognized this dichotomy, they were not perfect either. For example, the Constitution rightly acknowledged the equality of *all* men created in God's image, but, in practice, this was not extended to all races. Many of the framers deplored slavery but compromised on the issue to win ratification of the Constitution. This hideous institution, though not the cause of the Civil War, became an emotional issue that helped to distance the two factions of the country.

With increased trade and immigration came the influence of European philosophers such as Voltaire, Rousseau, and John Stuart Mills, who "created a code of morality based on self-interest." Mills believed individual interests superseded any consideration of God. "The only freedom which deserves the name is that of pursuing our own good in our own way."[8]

The French philosophy of Deism also began gaining a foothold in the United States and was eventually adopted under the label of Unitarianism. These philosophies blended well with the humanistic thought which dominated Europe and later came to be known as secular humanism. Deists believed that a Supreme being of some kind existed but that he did not enter into close relationships with man. It denounced the validity of the Bible or divine intervention and denied the importance of Judeo-Christian ethics.

Modern history books identify the majority of our Founding Fathers as Deists, but this is blatantly untrue. While a few may have adhered to that philosophy, most were professing Christians. The Declaration of Independence makes assertions regarding God's role and character that no Deist would utter. Such deliberate misrepresentations are part of a movement over the last few decades to rewrite history and downplay the Judeo-Christian influence in America's history.

Losing Ground

In time, the Civil War tore the country apart. The gold rush and rapid western migrations began to diminish the influence of Christianity. Another religious philosophy to filter into the states from Europe was the theory of evolution. Though touted as scientific, it did not meet any of the established scientific criteria to be classified as such. Evolutionary philosophies had been part of Eastern religions for centuries, and Darwin, who was a Universalist Unitarian minister, found they fit well with his own religious beliefs.

Darwin's version of evolution was quickly accepted by humanists who did not want to believe that man is a unique creation who owes his existence to the Creator. Man was an end unto himself and was no longer bound by the rules of a higher power. Within each person, the humanists taught, was the power to become perfect. These beliefs freed man to become his best. The goal of the humanists was to eradicate the concept of God and absolute values through education.

Humanism and the Schools

Humanistic thought had long dominated European schools. In America, the Christian influence was strong, and most schools were started by churches or communities with strong religious beliefs. Many children were tutored at home and then sent to universities such as Yale, Harvard, and Princeton, all of which had been started as seminaries.

The first significant entry of humanism into American education came through Dr. Horace Mann, the first secretary of the Massachusetts Board of Education. A Unitarian, Mann professed to be a Christian, yet denied the traditional doctrines of that faith, and was a "thorough believer in the perfectibility of man."[9] Education, he stressed, was a *right* of all children and should be guaranteed by the state, not the parents. It was society as a whole that bore responsibility for education and is the "real . . . godfather for all its children."[10] Education, not God, would be the salvation of mankind. He further stated:

> What the church has been for medieval man the public school must become for democratic and rational man. God will be replaced by the concept of the public good. . . . The common schools . . . shall create a more far-seeing intelligence and a pure morality than has ever existed among communities of men.[11]

In 1850, Mann convinced the American public that schools should be secularized and, as such, would solve all the problems of crime and poverty in one century.[12] The clergy of that day strongly opposed this move, protesting that an education based on transient values instead of absolute standards would not bring peace, but chaos.

The spread of this man-centered philosophy through the schools was slow at first. Local communities still exerted significant control over the public schools and curriculum. Gradually, compulsory attendance laws were passed throughout the states, and schooling was taken from the homes and churches and mandated into the public arena.

Then, John Dewey, the Father of Progressive Education, entered the scene. Dewey, who was a board member of the American Humanist Association when they drafted the first *Humanist Manifesto*, did more to bring humanism into the public schools than anyone else. "There is no God and there is no soul," he proclaimed and carried that belief into America's education system.[13] Dewey viewed the educator's role as "a social servant set apart for the maintenance of proper social order and the securing of the right social growth. . . . In this way the teacher is always the prophet of the true god and the usherer of the true kingdom of god."[14]

Still, the community had significant input into the local schools until 1957, when the federal government began giving federal aid to local schools, effectively negating local control.[15] Judeo-Christian influence began to slip radically, and, in 1962, God and prayer were expelled from America's public education system by the Supreme Court ruling in *Envel v. Vitale.* Under a broad interpretation of the "separation clause" (and a total disregard of the "free exercise clause") of the First Amendment, prayer was outlawed in American schools. Humanism, though officially a religion, was not banned.

The Proselytizing of America's Children

I am convinced that the battle for humankind's future must be waged and won *in the public school classroom* by teachers who correctly perceive their role as the proselytizers of a new faith; a religion of humanity that recognizes and respects what theologians call divinity in every human being . . . (emphasis in original).

The classrooms must and will become an arena of conflict between the old and the new—the rotting corpse of Christianity, together with all its adjacent misery, and the faith of Humanism, resplendent in its promise of a world in which the never-realized Christian idea of "love-thy-neighbor" will finally be achieved.[15]

Freed from the confines of traditional values, an all-out effort was launched to eradicate any remnant of Judeo-Christian influence and convert children to the philosophies embodied in *The Humanist Manifesto*.

In 1973, a Harvard University professor outlined the goals of modern education while speaking at a teacher's seminar: to eliminate allegiance to home and country, and to create universal children. He explained:

> Every child in America entering school at the age of five is mentally ill because he comes to school with certain allegiances toward our founding fathers, toward our elected officials, toward his parents, toward a belief in a supernatural being, toward the sovereignty of this nation as a separate entity. It's up to you teachers to make all of these sick children well by creating the international children of the future.[16]

The Radical Revolution

As the humanist philosophy permeated education, children were taught to reject the values of their parents and of society as a whole. There was no right and wrong. "God is dead!" the cover of *Time* announced. And, as Dostoyevsky observed, "Anything is permissible if there is no God." Without absolute standards, kids were left to develop their own values.

But, self-centered relativism does not create utopia—it breeds chaos. And, humanism, the ultimate religion of self, found chaotic expression in the cultural revolution of the 1960s. Students protested war, yet blew up school buildings. They screamed out against the hypocrisy and materialism of their parent's generation, yet shunned loving, monogamous relationships. Sex became more than a means of gratification, it became a weapon to break down all vestiges of moral barriers. Young people who got caught up in the peace movement were ridiculed for remaining chaste, or even remaining sexually faithful to one partner. They were encouraged to experiment with bisexual and homosexual behavior.

Having been taught that no absolutes exist, the radical Left movement sought to tear down all social systems which depicted values and order. Peter Collier and David Horowitz, who were editors of the New Left magazine *Ramparts*, describe the decade as

> a time when the "System"—that collection of values that provide guidelines for societies as well as individuals—was assaulted and mauled. As one center of authority after another was discredited under the New Left, we radicals claimed that we murdered to create. . . .
>
> In the attack against authority, we had weakened our culture's immune system, making it vulnerable to opportunistic diseases. The origins of the metaphorical epidemics of crime and drugs could be traced to the Sixties, as could literal ones such as AIDS.[17]

The war ended. Many of the leaders of the radical Left were in prison, Mexico, or dead. The rage that had spilled off the college campuses died down, but the legacy did not die with it.

The protesters grew up, got jobs, and went to Congress, carrying moral relativism into the most influential offices of the land. A few, like Collier and Horowitz, stepped back and "took inventory" of the legacy of this period. And, their conclusion?

"What have we learned by the middle of the journey? In brief, that the radical future is an illusion and that the American present is worth defending; that we were a part of a destructive generation whose work is not over yet."[18]

Humanism in Society

The influence of humanism spread to all segments of society but was perhaps most noticeable in the media and entertainment industries. In 1966, the movie industry threw out the Motion Picture Code, rules of ethics created by the industry in 1930. The code was based upon a recognition of "responsibility to the public because . . . entertainment and art are important influences in the life of a nation." Standards listed in the code were consistent with the values of society. For example:

- explicit sexual material was forbidden. Adultery and premarital sex were not to be presented as acceptable lifestyles.
- Religious leaders and beliefs were to be treated with respect.
- Obscenity of any kind was forbidden.
- The portrayal of violence would be limited. Brutal violence was not to be presented in detail.
- Children's sex organs could never be exposed.
- Seduction or rape should never be more than suggested.
- There was to be no hint of sexual perversions.

The code ended with the observation that "correct entertainment raises the whole standard of a nation. Wrong entertainment lowers the whole living condition and moral ideals of a race." Many within the movie industry had chaffed against these standards, which were not always consistently enforced. But, when the code was scrapped in 1966, the changes in the industry were drastic.

The Legacy

Tocqueville once asked, "How is it possible that society should escape destruction if the moral tie is not strengthened in proportion as the political tie is relaxed? And what can be done with a people who are their own masters if they are not submissive to the Deity?"[19]

A look at American society today can answer that question. A person's behavior is determined by his beliefs and values. The leading causes of death for young people are alcohol-related accidents, murder, and suicide. Children kill each other for their tennis shoes. Rape and other violent crimes are skyrocketing; sexually transmitted diseases have reached epidemic proportions. America has more divorces than any civilized country in the world. Thousands of babies are born each year addicted to crack or stricken with AIDS.

Pliney the Elder, a great Roman scholar, observed, "What we do to our children, they will do to society."[20] In our determination to be free from all constraints, we have stolen our children's moral heritage.

We are raising a lost generation.

2

The Lie of
Sexual Freedom

Until the 1960s, the teen-age pregnancy rate was steadily dropping as people began waiting until later to get married. While some teens did engage in premarital sex, they were in the minority. A belief in the value of monogamous relationships combined with a natural fear of unplanned pregnancies kept many young people from experimenting. But, in the sixties, society took a drastic swing. Traditional values were under assault and the ready availability of "The Pill" took away the fear of unpleasant consequences. A sexual revolution began which has left in its wake a legacy of personal and societal tragedy.

The answer, of course, was more sex education in the schools, easy access to contraceptives for teens, and the legalization of abortion to take care of any "accidents" that might occur. But, this has only fueled the problem. Since these "solutions" have been in place, "teenage sexual activity and teenage pregnancy have increased almost four hundred percent."[1] Polls taken of school-age children show that 56 percent of girls and 73 percent of boys report becoming sexually active by the age of eighteen, compared to 35 and 55 percent, respectively, in 1970.[2] Of those sexually active teens, 80 percent have had sex-ed courses and know how and where to acquire contraceptives, though only 40 percent admit using them on their first encounter.[3]

An even more troubling trend is the increasingly younger ages at which children are becoming sexually active. According to the Centers for Disease Control and Prevention (CDC), 40 percent of fifteen-year-olds also report having had sexual intercourse, as compared to 10 percent in 1970.[4] Most research indicates that the average age for a sexually active teen's first encounter was fourteen for boys and fifteen for girls.[5]

Many parents assume that if their children attend church regularly, then they will not become another statistic. Unfortunately, that is not the case. A study conducted by Josh McDowell's "Why Wait?" campaign showed that sexual activity among children who belonged to evangelical Christian denominations was only slightly less than that of nonchurched youth. The results: 65 percent of the eighteen-year-olds, 53 percent of the sixteen-year-olds, and 20 percent of the thirteen-year-olds in church youth groups had experienced sexual encounters.[6]

Kids Having Kids

Pregnancy rates among unwed teens are soaring. The CDC reports that "for more than a decade, the annual rate of unmarried U.S. teens having babies has gone up. In 1991 it was 44.8 births per 1,000; 11 years previously it was 27.6 per 1,000."[7] This year more than 1,100,000 teen-age girls will become pregnant in the United States, 83 percent of them unmarried—30,000 under the age of fourteen. The majority of these girls will become pregnant again within two years.

Of the over one million teen pregnancies, "about 400,000 will end in abortion, a 100 percent increase since 1972. Another 127,000 will end in miscarriage. Of the 490,000 births, 270,000 will be to unwed teens, a three-fold increase since 1960."[8] Ten percent of the teens who become pregnant do marry their partner, yet a marriage based on such shaky ground has numerous obstacles to overcome. Over half of such unions end in divorce within the first five years.[9]

Although sex education is mandated in forty-six states, and the majority of teen-agers are well-informed on the use of contraceptives, knowledge does not equate action, and only half of the teens surveyed used birth control during their first sexual encounter.[10]

Nor is birth control always effective, as Laticha Allen can testify. She was a virgin when she met her son's father, and when they became involved sexually they always used condoms. However, condoms have a 15 percent failure rate in preventing pregnancy (a fact often omitted from sex-ed curriculum), and Laticha still became pregnant. Her boyfriend stood by her during the pregnancy and childbirth and visits their son regularly, even contributing to his support. Yet, Laticha is facing life as a single parent.[11]

Kelly, a nineteen-year-old prelaw student, was using both condoms and birth control pills when she became pregnant. Already the parent of one child almost two years old, Kelly was upset with the news. "I was mad, really mad," Kelly said. "I want so much now for my child and for myself. I didn't want to add another one." Kelly chose to abort her baby.[12]

Someone to Love Me

Though most unwed teen mothers happened upon their state unintentionally, about one-fourth claim that they became pregnant on purpose. This is especially true in some poor neighborhoods

> where the traditional fears of getting pregnant or getting someone else pregnant are upside down. Teenage boys in these neighborhoods not only push the girls to have sex, they pressure them to have babies. The girls don't worry that they will get pregnant; they worry they *won't* (emphasis in original).[13]

If a boy's friends have fathered children and he hasn't, then he feels challenged to prove his virility. For some girls, getting pregnant is a way to keep a boyfriend. According to Cathy Mullen, nurse practitioner at East Side Health Center in Five Points, a poor district in Denver, Colorado, a lot of girls think getting pregnant is a way to obtain the attention they crave. " 'Instead of thinking ahead to 18 years of having to raise a child, they think their boyfriend will pay them attention for a little while' if they have a baby. . . . For others, it is as simple as 'wanting something of their own to love.' "[14]

Isabel was only fourteen when she discovered she was pregnant with her son. "Isabel, who says most of her friends in her west Denver neighborhood are pregnant or already mothers, says her pregnancy was a happy surprise."[15] The father, an unemployed, sixteen-year-old high school dropout, is a sore subject with the family, but the baby, Santiago Alfredo Huerta Sabreda, is the pride and joy of his mom, grandmother, and nineteen-year-old aunt.

Isabel's setting is far from unique. In Denver's

nineteen poorest neighborhoods, there is an average of one baby per girl before her twentieth birthday. And, in the thirty-two neighborhoods which house 41 percent of that city's poor, "four babies are born for every five teenage girls." Although some girls will not give birth, other teens will have two or more children before they come of age.[16]

The Cost

It is impossible to quantitatively measure the cost of teen pregnancy in terms of emotional damage and lost potential. Nor can you accurately measure the long-range impact of children being reared in single parent homes without the influence of a father. Most of the girls who chose to carry through the pregnancy decide to keep their babies. Seven out of ten of these mothers depend on welfare to support their child, costing the government approximately one hundred thousand dollars in medical and welfare expenses for the average child during the time that child remains in assistance. That does not include such things as government provided day care, foster care, housing, school lunches, etc., all of which prove there is nothing "free" about this kind of love.[17]

Many girls who do become teen mothers find it necessary to drop out of school to care for their child or to supplement their incomes. Unfortunately, this serves to trap them in a vicious cycle of poverty. Most adult women who go on Aid to Families with Dependent Children (AFDC) are able to become independent within two years, though over half will return to the rolls; the same is not true of teens. Without sufficient education and job skills to compete for anything more than minimum wage, they become trapped in a lifelong cycle of government dependence.

Isabel hopes to be an exception. With strong support from her family, she is continuing her education. Before having her child, she had dreams of becoming a veterinarian or a probation officer. This goal may be more difficult to attain, yet she continues to pursue it, getting an after-school job for now and planning to attend night school after graduation.[18]

Victims of Abortion

Not every pregnant teen, however, greets the news in the same manner as Isabel. Each year, almost half a million girls who find themselves in this condition fall prey to the abortion industry. In 1971, the United States Supreme Court cleared the way for the legal slaughter of unborn children with *Roe v. Wade*. The result has been a very lucrative industry that operates without oversight and few legal restraints.

Doctors are not allowed to remove infected toenails or perform routine physicals on a minor without parental consent. Yet, most states do not require parental notification for abortions, even though this surgery can cause serious injury or death. Since abortion is described as "birth control," the clinics who perform the procedure are allowed to operate without interference from medical inspections and regulations.

For example, before other surgeries, patients are given a full disclosure statement listing every conceivable thing that can go wrong up to and including death. Yet, young girls who are pressured into ending the life of their child are routinely lied to about the possible consequences. They are assured that the "fetus" is not a baby at all, but an unfeeling, unformed, insensitive mass of flesh. They are not warned of the risk of a perforated uterus, serious infection, sterility, and possible death. They are not told of the possibility that their breasts may fill with milk, leaving them guilt-ridden and longing to nurse a child who is no longer there. They do not warn them of the emotional damage suffered by so many other abortion survivors.

And, if a girl does survive the operation without apparent physical harm, the danger does not end there. Abortion patients are not warned that early abortions significantly increase their chances of getting breast cancer, a disease that kills one woman every fifteen minutes in America today. Prochoice groups tend to downplay this link, claiming that the studies are flawed and based solely on the memories of cancer patients (as though a woman would ever forget having an abortion !). Yet, this is not the case. More than twenty-four studies have proven the relationship between abortions and cancer, and some of those studies have been longitudinal, following a group of abortion patients for a long period of time, and therefore have not relied on memory at all.[19]

According to the available research, "women who have had miscarriages or abortions before a full-term pregnancy have a 50% greater chance of getting cancer than those who did not. The greater the number of miscarriages or abortions, the greater the risk."[20] Experience has proven this to be true. In the Soviet Union, contraceptives were difficult to obtain, so abortions became commonly used as birth control. During this period, from 1960 to 1987, breast cancer among women in Russia, Estonia, and Georgia tripled. In 1970, Washington State began to provide public funding for abortions for the indigent. The result: breast cancer among the poor soared by 53 percent, while the rate for wealthy women in the same area dropped by 1 percent.[21]

In spite of the evidence, four hundred thousand teens each year choose (or are pressured into) abortions without any warning that the decision could result in a painful, potentially fatal disease later in life.

Deadly Consequences

Another legacy of "sexual freedom" has been a virtual epidemic of sexually transmitted diseases, or STDs. Twenty years ago, there were two major STDs: syphilis and gonorrhea. Because of newly discovered antibiotics, these were considered under control. But in the sixties, they came back with a vengeance as new strains mutated, immune to the drugs which had been so effective. In addition, new diseases began appearing. Now there are twenty-seven known STDs, with a new one being discovered approximately every nine months.[22]

Sexually transmitted diseases occur more frequently than any other category of infectious disease in the United States.[23] There are over thirteen million reported new cases of STDs each year in this country, and one-fourth of them are in teenagers. That means that one out of four kids will have a sexually transmitted disease before graduating from high school.[24] The highest rate of incidence occurs in children between the ages of ten and nineteen. Sixty-five percent of all reported cases occur in young people under the age of twenty-five.[25] For young women, this can be especially unfortunate, since sterility is a common side effect of STDs in females. Young women just starting out in their first relationships may be condemning themselves to a future where they can't even think about having children.

Over forty-three million Americans have been diagnosed with an STD—one in five—and the number is rising. In spite of this, Americans appear woefully naive about the dangers of casual sex. According to some surveys, as many as 75 percent of adults believe that they cannot contract a STD, even though many of those same respondents admitted they were not in monogamous relationships.[26] There are a couple of reasons for this cavalier attitude. One is the current "safe sex" propaganda, and the other is ignorance about the extent of STDs. The high visibility of AIDS has left many young people thinking that it is the only disease that should concern them. Those who do not participate in bisexual or homosexual activity or use IV drugs mistakenly think they are safe, especially if they use the condoms handed out with such abandon at some schools today.

Know Your Partner

Another recommendation made by the CDC and sex education organizations is that you "know your partner." Find out if they have participated in homosexual or IV drug activities and how many partners they have had in the past. But, this advice is less than practical since most sexually active teens are uncomfortable about offending their partner by asking such questions. Also, it is based upon the assumption that people are likely to tell the truth about such intimate details. But, surveys taken on college campuses reveal that young men intent upon a "score" often do lie about their past activities. In one study, 34 percent of the college men interviewed admitted that they had lied in order to have sex. In another study, 50 percent of the men and 40 percent of the women said they would lie regarding the number of past partners, and 20 percent of the men admitted they would lie about having been tested for AIDS.

But, even if a date tells the truth, knowing your partner is not enough. When two people have intercourse, they are not only involving one another, but they are also having intercourse with every partner the other person has had for the last ten years and their partner's partners, etc. Those prospects alone make a great case for chastity!

Condoms Not Enough

While condoms do offer some protection, they are far from safe. When used as birth control, they fail 15 percent of the time, even when used properly. This is a significant percentage when you consider that although pregnancy can only occur a few days a month, you can catch diseases any day. In protecting against AIDS, only the latex condoms have any effectiveness, and reports in the *New England Journal of Medicine*, and the *American Medical Association Journal* reveal the unreliability of these as well. Studies were conducted among married couples in which one partner was diagnosed with HIV. The results were tragic. Three out of ten infected partners transmitted the disease to their mates within twenty-four months, even though condoms were used 100 percent of the time. Considering that the average incubation period for this virus is eight years, the numbers could go even higher.[27]

Another fact that former Surgeon General Jocelyn Elders failed to tell the public during her tireless condom campaign, is that for many sexually transmitted diseases, condoms offer absolutely *no* protection. Syphilis, for example, can be passed through deep, or French, kissing if a person has a lesion in his mouth. In fact, contact with sores or lesions on any part of the body, such as the finger or breast or any broken place on your skin, can spread the disease.[28] Additionally, condoms offer no protection against herpes and genital warts and only limited protection against gonorrhea and chlamydia.

STDs: The Consequences

The following chart shows the rate of infection in the United States for the eight most common STDs.

Chlamydia—4,000,000 cases per year
Gonorrhea—1,300,000 cases per year
Genital Warts—1,000,000 cases per year
Genital Herpes—500,000 cases per year
PID—420,000 cases treated per year (There
    may be more untreated cases.)
Hepatitis B—300,000 cases per year
Syphilis—134,000 cases per year
AIDS—242,145 total AIDS cases through Oc-
    tober 1992; 1.5 million HIV positive.[29]

Unfortunately, these numbers continue to rise, and each number represents a person whose life has been irreparably damaged. The heartbreaking impact is illustrated in this letter written by a young lady.

It took losing my virginity at a very young age, losing my self-respect and possibly my fertility, helping to ruin another person's marriage and family life, acquiring a non-curable virus, not getting the fulfillment that sex should provide in marriage . . . for me to realize how detrimental sex before marriage can really be.[30]

The National Institutes of Health (NIH) estimate that more than twenty-five million Americans suffer from genital herpes, with another one-half million cases occurring each year. Women who have herpes must have Cesarean deliveries if they have children, or the babies will become infected, and perhaps blinded, by the disease. Some studies even indicate that herpes and genital warts increase the risk of cervical cancer.

Gonorrhea, which has an incredible ability to become resistant to antibiotics, is developing into superstrains that may become untreatable. Dr. John W. Boslego of Walter Reed Army Institute of Research in Washington, D.C., warns, "We are beginning to run out of drugs. We are rapidly approaching the years when the medical profession could end up with no drugs able to fight certain strains of this ancient crippler and sterilizer."[31]

The most common form of STD is chlamydia, affecting more than four million Americans annually. The largest group carrying this disease are young men and women between the ages of fifteen and twenty-four.[32] What makes this disease so difficult is that it often has no noticeable initial symptoms. About 80 percent of the women who become infected do not notice any changes until the disease has progressed. Untreated, the disease can travel to the reproductive organs, causing infections and sterility. If it occurs within the cervix, it can cause pelvic inflammatory disease, or PID. And, PID, which may also be caused by gonorrhea, is a leading cause of sterility. Nearly one-fifth of PID patients are teenagers, and girls who have more than one sex partner are at greatest risk.[33]

Infants are also paying a high price for sexual freedom. In 1987, more babies were born with birth defects caused by STDs than the total number of children crippled by the ten-year polio epidemic of the 1950s.[34] Some children can be spared by a Cesarean delivery if the mother is aware of her disease. But, for babies born to HIV mothers, there is no protection. These babies are destined for a short life and painful death.

AIDS: The Deadly Scourge

In 1986, Rae Lewis-Thornton was a young, healthy professional just stopping by the Red Cross office to donate blood. But, the Red Cross didn't want her donation—she tested HIV positive. Nine years later, she describes her situation:

> I'm young—32. Well educated. Professional.

> Attractive. Smart. I've been drug- and alcohol-free all my life. I'm a Christian. I've never been promiscuous. Never had a one night stand. And I'm dying of AIDS.

> I've been living with the disease for nine years, and people still tell me that I am too pretty and intelligent to have AIDS. But I do. . . .

> I have no idea who infected me or when it happened.

> Still, there is one thing I am absolutely certain of: I am dying now because I had one sexual partner too many. And I'm here to tell you one is all it takes.[35]

AIDS first appeared in the homosexual community in the 1980s, but it has spread into all segments of society. The virus was simultaneously identified in the United States and France in 1983. By the end of September 1990, more than 152,000 people in the United States had been diagnosed with full-blown AIDS, and almost 94,000 had already died of the disease. Thousands more carried the HIV virus which causes AIDS, many unaware. Not everyone who has HIV will get AIDS, yet they are still capable of infecting others who may very well die of the disease. In addition, HIV is capable of hiding in a body cell completely undetected for up to six months. Once the body identifies the intruder and the immune system begins to attack, the virus simply mutates and becomes unrecognizable again. The virus is even thought to be able to lay dormant for as long as ten years before beginning its slow, destructive work.

And, the number of victims keeps increasing. In New York City, AIDS is the leading cause of death in both men and women in their twenties.[36] It is also the leading cause of death in African-American and Hispanic adolescent women in both New York and New Jersey.[37] C. Everett Koop, former surgeon general under Reagan, estimates that between fifty and one hundred million people will die of AIDS globally by the end of the century.[38]

As the age of sexual activity gets younger, so does the age of infection with HIV. Many of the people who are currently being diagnosed with AIDS are between twenty and twenty-five, which means that they probably became infected as teens. "The CDC estimates that as many as 25% of these people were infected between the ages of 13 and 19."[39] In fact, over the last few years, the number of children under the age of nineteen diagnosed with full-blown AIDS has doubled every fourteen months. The speed at which this epidemic has spread is alarming. The first five cases were reported in 1981. It took a little over eight years, from June of 1981 to August of 1989, for the first one hundred thousand cases in the United States to be reported. But then, in just a little over two years, the number doubled.

The rate of increase is so alarming that it prompted Dr. Koop to comment that this was a plague which could conceivably wipe out an entire generation. The sexual revolution promised freedom: it delivered death.

3

Drunk, Drugged, and Dropping Out

A 1983 Volvo raced down Titan Road filled with six teen-agers heading home from a party. The bright headlight of an approaching coal train signaled the upcoming railroad tracks. The driver, who was drunk, stepped on the gas, apparently trying to beat the train. Seconds later, these vibrant, active teen-agers were statistics.[1]

Alcohol, America's drug of choice, is killing our kids. Over thirty-six hundred die as a result of drinking and driving each year, and another eighty-five thousand are injured. According to the National Council on Alcoholism, this is the leading killer of young people between the ages of fifteen and twenty-four.

Teen alcoholism is also on the rise. In one survey of twenty-seven thousand public school students, 11 percent expressed a belief that they could not control their drinking. It is now estimated that 3.3 million young people between the ages of fourteen and seventeen show signs of alcoholism.[2] In 1987, Secretary of Health and Human Services Otis Bowen claimed nearly five million adolescents had drinking problems. Part of the blame, he said, should be laid at the feet of brewers and beer distributors who spend $15 million to $20 million each year marketing their products to young people.[3]

Not only are kids drinking more, but the age at which they begin is also lower. A survey of fourth graders revealed that one in three had been pressured to drink wine coolers, and 25 percent had acquiesced. By sixth grade, 40 percent of the students reported having consumed alcohol—an increase of almost 150 percent over the last six years.[4] Substance abuse counselors report that it is not unusual to see children as young as ten with serious drinking problems.

The destructive impact this situation has on such young lives is hard to measure. When a person develops a dependency on alcohol, the natural emotional development ceases. During the years they should be learning self-government, conflict resolution, and stress-managing skills, they learn to numb their senses instead. Substance abuse also affects learning and mental and physical development. Alcohol suppresses the rational part of the brain and relaxes normal inhibitions, which is why it is often associated with a teen's first sexual encounter. Invariably, when young people do lose their virginity in this manner the experience is less than satisfying, often leaving them embarrassed and feeling used.

Justice Department statistics have also tied alcohol use to 37 percent of all youth crime. For example, drinking is connected to

- 27 percent of all murders;
- 33 percent of all property offenses;

- 31 percent of all rapes; and
- 33 to 60 percent of all date rapes.[5]

Following Society's Footsteps

Every day Americans consume 15.7 million gallons of beer and ale, or 28 million six-packs, enough to fill a football stadium thirty feet deep in beer cans. On top of that we use 1.2 million gallons of hard liquor, or enough to make 26 million people seriously drunk.[6] It's no wonder young people have problems with alcohol; they are simply following the adults' example. Society continually bombards them with the message that drinking is glamorous, a sign of maturity, and a necessary ingredient for happiness. And, if everybody's doing it, what's wrong?

But, alcohol abuse is a national tragedy. Half of those who die on our highways do so because of drunk drivers. According to the American Hospital Association, half of all hospital admissions are alcohol related. And, alcohol is often an ingredient in domestic abuse and other forms of violence and crime. In fact, half of all the murders and suicides in the United States have some connection to alcohol.

Kids and Chemicals

The problem with chemical abuse is not only confined to alcohol and illicit substances; there is a proliferation of prescription drugs being used to correct and manipulate behavior, weight, sleeplessness, and a myriad of other conditions. Rather than finding and treating the cause for these problems, we too often fight the symptoms with drugs.

One current fad is the treatment of attention deficit/hyperactivity disorder, or ADHD. Though this is a genuine condition in a few children, it is now the diagnosis of choice for any child who does not fit into a so-called norm.

> Those formerly labeled "late bloomers" are now "developmentally delayed," boys who once had "ants in their pants" are diagnosed with attention deficit disorder. "Everybody's got a disability," says school psychologist Kevin Dwyer, N.C.S.P., a member of the National Joint Commission for Learning Disabilities.[7]

The list of "indicators" of ADHD has grown to the point that almost any child could be diagnosed and drugged. For example, forgetfulness in daily activities, a trademark of childhood, and talking excessively are both listed as indicators. The American Academy of Child and Adolescent Psychiatry also lists the common childhood complaints of fearfulness, aggression, and separation anxiety as "disorders" warranting drugs. There seems to be a movement to create the perfect child through chemicals.

Though only doctors can prescribe these medications, they rely heavily upon questionnaires filled out by teachers. And, too often, the teachers know exactly what to write down to get the desired treatment. It is much easier to sedate a bored middle school student who is boisterous and struggling in school because he has never been taught to read properly. One teacher told a mother that her daughter had ADHD simply because she was in the bottom third of the class: so much for individuality. Children are creative creatures and known to daydream, yet a child who daydreams in class may now be sent to the school psychiatrist for evaluation.

Under this criteria, Thomas Edison and Albert Einstein would have both been put on Ritalin.

That does not mean that there are not a few children with ADHD. But, drugs should be used only in extreme cases and as a last resort. Some people have been very effective fighting this problem with diet and nutrition. But, our public schools no longer recognize the parents' right to seek medical treatment of their choice. Many parents who have refused to drug their children, and have chosen other more effective ways of dealing with their behavior, have suddenly found themselves in danger of losing their children under charges of medical or emotional neglect. It is not uncommon for a teacher who does not approve of the parents' choice of options to simply call in the local Child Protection Agency. In numerous cases, untrained and unqualified social workers will threaten removal of the child from the home if the parent does not comply with the teacher's desired treatment.

Drugs Not Safe

When drugs such as Valium, Prozac, and Ritalin are prescribed to young children, parents are not always made aware of the potentially debilitating side effects which may accompany their use. Valium can cause depressed appetite, weight loss, listlessness, and excruciating headaches. When Ritalin wears off, many children "crash," and become even more uncontrollable than they were before. In addition, it can cause insomnia, stomach pain, and weight loss. Other popular drugs can cause intestinal and stomach pain, headaches, faintness, and heart-racing.[8] Many of these drugs are also addictive and can put their children at risk for illicit drug use once the prescriptions stop.

One child in Washington, D.C., was diagnosed by three doctors with ADHD before he was put on Ritalin. But, within seventy-two hours, the child began groaning and twitching. One doctor believes the Ritalin may have given him a neurological disorder called Tourette's syndrome, which is characterized by persistent tics. The child was then switched to Desipramine, which sent him into rages and increased his heart rate to a frightening level. He stayed on this medication until four other children on Desipramine who had no history of heart disease died of heart attacks. The next choice was Catapres, which left the little boy weepy and depressed. Finally, he was placed on Prozac, which only makes his ears red.[9]

Parents are also unaware that 80 percent of the drugs being prescribed for children have only been tested and approved for adults. Dr. Gloria Troendle of the FDA says, "You're really experimenting on them [children] every time you give them a drug."[10]

One example of this is Prozac, a very popular drug introduced in 1988 and commonly prescribed for children. Ritalin, which is labeled for children, is still not being prescribed properly. The *Physicians' Desk Reference* specifically states, "Warning. . . . Ritalin should not be used in children under six years, since safety and efficacy in this age group have not been established." In spite of this, over two hundred thousand prescriptions for stimulates were written in 1993 for children five-years-old and under.[11]

Leon Eisenberg, M.D., of Harvard Medical School strongly recommends that drugs only be used in extreme cases. In recent studies, half of the children examined did no better on drugs than on placebos. Dr. Eagle expresses concern that drugging a child interferes with his natural emotional development. "Kids do bad, messy, unattractive things—part of their development is to learn to control their impulses, which parents can help them do. Kids given drugs won't learn how to do that." He also expressed concern that what was being diagnosed as a "disability" is often nothing more than a difference in personalities. "There's a place for different personalities because there are different paths in life. We shouldn't pathologize difference."[12]

Drugging America

Every day

- Americans snort 325 pounds of cocaine, enough to fill a bathtub.
- Five thousand Americans try cocaine for the first time, many of them children.
- Americans smoke 85,000 pounds of marijuana, a bale about the size of a small house.
- Police arrest five hundred busloads of people; 70 percent of them have illegal drugs in their possession.
- Fifty-six million American families battle with alcohol problems, costing $116 billion per year.
- Americans go to sleep with the help of thirty million sleeping pills. Valium now outsells aspirin.[13]

We have become one of the most violent, crime-ridden industrial nations in the world. We are also the world's biggest consumer of illegal narcotics. With only 5 percent of the world's population, we still consume a staggering 50 percent of the world's annual cocaine output.[14]

Drug addiction reached epidemic proportions in this country during the 1960s. Over the next two decades that followed, the problem seemed to level off and even begin to decline. Unfortunately, drugs are once more on the rise, due in large part to the introduction of crack, the "poor man's" version of cocaine. Unlike cocaine, however, crack gives an instant high and is one of the most addictive drugs available. It is also extremely deadly.

Prior to June of 1985, New York police had never made a single arrest for crack possession. During the first ten months of 1988, they had already made 19,074 such arrests. Gangs operating as crack distributors in Los Angeles were responsible for 387 murders in 1987. In Atlanta that same year deaths due to cocaine overdoses jumped 250 percent, and in Philadelphia cocaine deaths increased 259 percent.[15] As the price for crack dropped from forty dollars to fifteen, it quickly became a drug of choice for many young people. One school district in Detroit banned pagers in an attempt to restrict the sale of drugs.

Studies also indicate that the age of first drug use is also dropping. Marijuana use, often a first step into drug abuse, has more than doubled among eighth-grade students since 1991. Additionally, one-fourth of these student admitted they had used an illegal drug at least once, a 10 percent increase over the year before.[16]

Some people, such as former Surgeon General Jocelyn Elders, believe the solution is to decriminalize drugs, but such a notion is ludicrous. Drugs kill, period. Not only do they kill the person taking them, they destroy other innocent lives as well. Legalization would simply be an admission of defeat.

Dropping Out

Every thirty minutes in the United States,

- 29 kids will attempt suicide;
- 57 adolescents will run away;
- 685 teenagers will use some form of narcotic;
- 188 young people will abuse alcohol.[17]

We are raising a generation of children that seem to have given up on their future. For some kids, the road to addiction began with nothing more than a desire to fit in with the crowd. For others, drugs and alcohol are a way to hide from the pain of loneliness, of poor self-worth, or fractured families. Some children chose to drop out of school, of home, or even life.

Life on the Streets

I do not consider myself to be a follower, just a lonely, deserted soul in a barbaric city, who walks his own treacherous path in life.

—Written by Brian, after six months alone on the street.[18]

They hang out on main drags in major cities; unknown faces that work the streets at night or slip into shelters, trying to blend in with the surroundings. Some ask for refuge in gang houses. These are America's street kids, children who have run away or been thrown out of their homes.

Each year approximately 1.3 million teen-agers leave home. While accurate numbers are hard to come by, those who work at youth shelters, such as New York-based Covenant House, find the numbers are growing and the kids are getting younger.

Among the top destinations for kids are San Francisco, Seattle, New York City, and Los Angeles. In Los Angeles County alone it is estimated that there are ten thousand homeless kids on the streets each night, with about a third of them in Hollywood.[19]

The reasons young people leave home vary. A few run away out of rebellion or because of the lure of excitement independence offers or because of conflicts over drug use. Some leave to avoid the typical parent-teen conflicts.

For a growing number of Southeast Asian kids, leaving home is a way to deal with clashing cultures. For all adolescents, the pressure to conform to peers is great, but this is especially true for immigrants. Parents cannot understand why their children reject their cultural heritage, while teens cannot understand why their parents seem so backward. Noc, a fifteen-year-old Cambodian refugee, ran away because his parents wouldn't let him pierce his ear.[20]

Most of the Asian runaways are not on the streets, however, but live in a loose network of "crash pads," small houses or apartments rented by large numbers of teen-agers. Because most Asian refugees come from countries where government officials could not be trusted, most of these runaways are never reported. But, counselors in Seattle, where there is a large Asian population, estimate that one third of all refugee families in that area have had a child run away.[21]

Law enforcement officers have become increasingly concerned about the Asian runaways, noting that when the money runs out, those too young for jobs generally turn to crime. Also, these kids are prime candidates to be recruited by Asian gangs.

Exchanging Hostilities for Horror

An increasing number of children are leaving home to escape abuse. Many leave to escape their parents' alcohol or drug problems, physical or emotional abuse, or even sexual molestation. Mary Rose McGeady, president of Covenant House, tells of a disturbing trend of children as young as ten being used to run drugs for their parents. More and more, these frightened kids are appearing at the shelter, pockets filled with drugs, and automatic pistols in their coats.

Child protection agencies are supposed to help children like this, but many times they fall through the cracks. And, those placed in foster care are ten times more likely to be abused or molested than children in the general population. For some kids, the streets seem preferable. In 1988, social workers in Cumberland County, Oregon, went public with the information that 150 children officially living in state custody were actually on the streets or in unapproved, abusive settings. Examples included:

- an eleven-year-old girl who was living on the streets;

- a thirteen-year-old boy who had been moved over twenty times in foster care and was now living with an older man, and possibly engaged in prostitution;

- a sixteen-year-old boy who had completed a jail sentence but was required to remain there for lack of a better place; and

- a pregnant, sexually abused seventeen-year-old who was living with an abusive male prostitute.[22]

But, kids who flee to the streets often find they have traded the hostilities at home for even greater horrors. Young, inexperienced, and unable to support themselves, they become caught up in a life of theft, drugs, and prostitution. Because of their lifestyles, street kids are at great risk for contracting HIV, and a growing number of them are beginning to die of AIDS. Some teens, like Al, find help too late. When Al came to the shelter in New York, he appeared to be fine; but workers soon discovered his secret—he was dying of AIDS. In time, he shared his story, one they had heard before. He had come to them, he said, because "dying in here is better than living outside."

> I mean, I never felt like I was alive when I was outside. I never had a father growing up, and my mother . . . my mother never wanted me. I can't remember ever being hugged, ever being told I was loved, ever feeling wanted.
>
> Then, about two years ago, my mother abandoned me in the middle of the night, and I was homeless. I've spent the last two years on the street, knowing what it's like to be hungry, and beaten, and used and bought and sold. Do you call that living?[23]

Al died at Covenant House. Finally, among strangers, he had found people who loved him.

The Final Solution

> Breaking laws, knocking doors but there's no one at home, made your bed, rest your head, but you lie there and moan. Where to hide, Suicide is the only way out. Don't you know what it's really about?[24]

John McCollum put on his favorite record, slipped the headphones on, and laid back in bed. As he listened to Ozzy scream out these words from "Suicide Solution," John put a gun to his head and pulled the trigger.[25]

Disillusioned with life, some young people are dropping out, permanently. Approximately three hundred thousand children will attempt suicide this year—at least six thousand will succeed. For the last twenty-five years, deaths by suicide have declined in all age brackets except one: ages fifteen to twenty-four. Teen suicide has tripled since 1950, and suicide deaths for children under fifteen have also tripled in the last thirty years. As a result, suicide has become the third leading cause of death for adolescents, and the second leading killer of college students.[26]

An extensive study on teen suicide revealed that the rate of attempts has skyrocketed from ten per one thousand to eight per one hundred. The problem has become so alarming that a representative from the Centers of Disease Control (CDC) observed, "If people in society were dying from a disease at the same rate that teenagers are dying from suicide, it would be considered a major epidemic."[27]

What is it that causes people at the very threshold of life to destroy themselves? The individual reasons are as varied as the people themselves, but there are some underlying similarities. Alcohol and drugs are a factor in half of all suicides. Many teens attempt suicide after a personal crisis, yet others suffer the same difficulties without choosing to end their lives, indicating that the real issues lie deeper.

In a 1991 Gallop Poll, teen suicide survivors gave the following reasons for their attempts.

Family problems.................. 47 percent
Depression............................ 23 percent
Problems with friends......... 22 percent
Low self-esteem.................... 18 percent
Boy/girl relationships......... 16 percent
Feeling no one cares........... 13 percent[28]

Though there are many causes, the majority of
teens who attempt suicide live in fractured families
and suffer from a feeling of isolation. The dramatic
increase in teen suicide strongly parallels the disintegration of the family and the abandonment of
faith in a personal God. In 1950, when teen suicide
was a rare occurrence, most children grew up in
homes with two parents and received some spiritual
training. Now, 27 percent of America's teen-agers
live in single parent homes, and 74 percent have
mothers who work outside the home. The majority
of families no longer attend church weekly as a
family, and God has been expelled from the public
schools. Without a strong spiritual foundation, or
close family ties, many kids feel completely alone
and powerless to fill the void.

Today, 843 American teen-agers will attempt a
final solution to their pain: 17 will succeed.

4

An Epidemic of Violence

Twelve-year-old Cindy Rodriquez stands talking to the mailman in her front yard in South Central Los Angeles. Suddenly, a stray gang bullet cuts through her body. Now, she is paralyzed for life.

In the affluent community of Glen Ridge, New Jersey, a mentally impaired girl is gang raped. Those accused of the crime are eight members of the football team.

Two Denver, Colorado, teens get into a fist fight. One boy pulls out a kitchen knife and stabs the other boy in the heart. The fifteen-year-old victim survives; the fourteen-year-old assailant awaits trial as an adult.

News stories such as these appear daily across the nation, revealing a virtual epidemic of youth violence and prompting many to wonder if we are raising a lost generation. Statistics from the U.S. Justice Department confirm that this perception has not just been caused by sensationalistic reporting. Since 1983, murders committed by juveniles under the age of eighteen have increased three times, rapes two times, and robberies five times. Homicide is now the leading killer of black males aged fifteen to twenty-four and the second-leading cause for white youths after car accidents.[1]

Murder now accounts for more deaths among teens than all diseases combined. And, the perpetrators are getting younger. In 1991, 17 percent of those arrested for violent crimes were between the ages of ten and seventeen. In 1992, one hundred thousand young people were arrested for violent crimes. Law enforcement officials believe that number is even higher now. "We're talking about younger and younger kids committing more and more serious crimes," says Indianapolis prosecuting Attorney Jeff Modisett.[2] The National Council on Crime and Delinquency reports that one hundred thousand adolescents are confined in correctional institutions on any given day, almost double the number of youth prisoners in 1975, even though the juvenile population dropped by six and one-half million in the last twenty years. Approximately thirty-eight are on death row.

Living in a War Zone

The majority, but by no means all, of these crimes occur in the inner city, where victim and perpetrator live side by side. In some neighborhoods, gunfire is a daily occurrence. In a poll conducted by *Newsweek*, one out of six young people between the ages of ten and seventeen had either seen or known someone who had been shot.[3] Counselors report dealing with increasing numbers of cases of post-traumatic syndrome in young children, something you would expect to see in Beirut, not America.

For many children, detachment is the best weapon against fear, resulting in an almost casual attitude toward violence. This is how six-year-old Shaakara, a girl from Chicago's Uptown, deals with her encounter with murder. She relates:

> "This lady, she got shot and her little baby had got cut. This man, he took the baby and cut her. He cut her on the throat. He killed the baby. All blood came out. This little boy, when he saw the baby, he called the grandmother and she came over. And you know, his grandmother got killed, but the little boy didn't get killed. He comes over to my house. That man, he took the grandmother and put her on the ground, and slammed her, and shut her in the door." After telling her tale, Shaakara smiles. "You know what I want to be when I grow up? A ballerina or a mermaid."[4]

Guns and Power

Children who grow up in such an atmosphere live in genuine fear for their lives. When one teacher in an inner city elementary school asked her students to write an essay about what they would like to be when they grow up, a young boy looked at her thoughtfully and replied, "To be alive." For many kids, the answer is to arm themselves. But, it can be very difficult for a child to draw the line between defensive and aggressive acts.

The teen-age love affair with guns is not just a phenomenon of the inner cities, however. Regardless of where they live, to immature kids, guns represent power, respect, and status. Larry Roberts, assistant police chief in Omaha, traces that city's surge in youth crime to 1986, when Los Angeles gang members moved into the area. Local teens began to compete with gang members for status, and the arms race was on. " 'If one kid brings a little .22-cal. pistol and the other has a .357 Magnum, then guess who has status' Roberts says. . . . 'For some reason this particular generation of kids has absolutely no value for human life. . . . They don't know what it is to die or what it means to pull the trigger.' "[5]

The Center for Health Statistics claims that 25 percent of all teen deaths are caused by gunshot wounds, including homicide, suicide and accidental deaths. A Harris poll of 2,508 students from 96 schools [polled] in the sixth through 12th grades said they have carried a handgun in the past 30 days, 11% said they have been shot at, and 59% said they know where to get a gun if they need one.[6]

Public and political response has been a move to restrict or even ban guns, a method which has been tried and failed. Laws restricting juvenile access to guns are common, but kids are still armed. Between 1987 and 1991, there was a 62 percent increase in juvenile arrests for weapons violations. Three times as many black youths were arrested for weapons than white youths in 1991, and the homicide rate for black teens was six times greater than for whites.[7]

Some of the most violent cities in our nation, such as Washington, D.C., and Chicago, have the toughest gun restrictions, yet those laws have done absolutely nothing to slow down the violence. Handgun sales were completely outlawed in Chicago in 1982, yet inner-city youths report that it takes less than two hours to procure any weapon they choose, and the increase in crime continues.[8] One of the reasons these laws fail is that they do not address the causes of violence. Guns are only a symptom: violence is a disease of the heart.

Safe in the Suburbs?

Armed with an automatic pistol and a double-action revolver, a sixteen-year-old boy in rural Montana holds two teen-agers hostage at school.

Angry at being expelled, a young student walks into a parochial school classroom, shoots the principal, and turns the gun on himself.

A Colorado state patrolman stops two youths on a mountain road for a traffic violation. The boys, who are driving a stolen vehicle, panic. One kid pulls a gun, and the veteran patrolman dies after calling for help. The two boys convicted of the crime are from the upscale Highlands Ranch community.

There is nothing new about youth violence, but in the past it was confined mainly to inner cities. Those who could afford to move did so in a wave of suburban migration. There, in quiet neighborhoods with well-staffed schools, families felt safe. That illusion of safety was shattered in Benson, a quiet Omaha suburb, when a seven-minute gunfight exploded in a white middle-class neighborhood. Miraculously, no one was killed, though two teens were injured—one seriously. Until that time, most Omaha residents considered shootings a problem confined to poor, black neighborhoods. Bonnie Elseman, a single mother whose son was involved in the episode, felt the same way.

> I've lived in this area all my life, and now boys are shooting at each other for the — — of it. . . . I now realize that I owe the blacks in Omaha an apology for ignoring all the shootings because I thought it was just their problem. I could just weep for all these kids."[9]

Even though small towns and rural areas *are* safer than the cities, no neighborhood is immune from the onslaught of youth violence. Crimes, such as murder, rape, assault, and robbery, jumped 30 percent in the suburbs between 1985 and 1991; many of the perpetrators were juveniles.

Violence and the Schools

While sending a child to school is still a better option than letting them run on the streets, numerous surveys reveal escalating levels of violence in public schools. In the forties and fifties "talking, chewing gum, making noise, running in the halls, getting out of turn in line, wearing improper clothing, and not putting paper in wastebaskets" were reported by teachers as the most pressing discipline problems they faced. By 1982, however, the list of offenses had changed drastically, including "rape, robbery, assault, burglary, arson, bombings, and murder."[10] In 1993, public schools were the scene of more than three million crimes. Law enforcement officials estimate 270,000 guns go to school each day, and more than 25 percent of all high school seniors report being threatened with violence.[11]

For many students, school has become a hostile environment where survival may depend on not wearing the wrong color. Even the most innocent behavior can be misconstrued as an insult and result in violence. Kara, a fifteen-year-old sophomore, explains, "You bump someone by accident, and they think you did it on purpose. They either shove you back, or they threaten to get you later. And if a gang member thinks you've insulted him, he'll come after you with a gun."[12]

At one time, perceived insults such as these were resolved with fists after school. Now, they are often resolved permanently. Two Massachusetts students charged into a classroom and shot a fifteen-year-old rival. An honor student in Kentucky, angry over a grade, marched into school and shot his teacher and a school janitor. In New York, two teens get into a shouting match, and one is shot to death. A group of Miami high school boys began arguing over a girl. At least three guns were pulled, and eighteen-year-old Conroy Robinson was dead. The coroner reported more than a dozen bullet holes in his body.

And, students are not the only ones in danger. In New York City alone, the United Federation of Teachers reported 2,790 crimes against teachers during the 1989–1990 school year. At least one-third of those involved assaults, robberies, and sexual offenses. In Detroit, attacks on teachers increased 990 percent over a five-year period.[13] But, these conditions do not just exist in major cities.

> In Abilene, Texas, a high school student shot a teacher in the head for giving him a low grade; in Florida's Pinellas County, a student killed an assistant high school principal and injured another administrator and teacher; in Goddard, Kansas, a fourteen-year-old boy gunned down two teachers and a junior high school principal; in Fort Worth, Texas, a teacher was stabbed to death and a twelve-year-old student confessed to the crime.[14]

In an effort to protect students and teachers alike, school districts are spending millions of dollars on armed guards, metal detectors, and other security measures. Some schools have enforced strict dress codes to reduce student thefts and gang rivalry. But, turning schools into armed camps is not the answer. Students cannot learn as well in a disruptive, potentially violent setting.

Killer Kids

Law enforcement officers nationwide have become increasingly alarmed by the changing character and age of juvenile criminals. A complete disrespect for life, a perverse viciousness, and an almost total lack of remorse make many criminologists wonder if we have raised a generation of sociopaths. The number of children killed for their athletic shoes, jewelry, or team jackets has so alarmed some schools that students are no longer allowed to wear these items on campus.

In Atlanta, fifty-five-year-old Charles Conrad surprised three teen-agers—ages fourteen, fifteen, and seventeen—burglarizing his condo. Confined to a wheelchair and suffering from multiple sclerosis, Conrad posed no physical threat to the teens, yet they decided to kill him anyway. Unfortunately for Conrad, he did not die easily. Over a period of several hours they stabbed him with a knife and barbecue fork, strangled him with a rope, and beat his head with a hammer and shotgun. After working up an appetite, the three took a break to raid the kitchen. According to a statement given by the youngest participant, the wounded victim pleaded with his assailants to shoot him and let him die. But, the kids were afraid of waking the neighbors, so the beatings continued.

After a time, Charles Conrad became silent. To make certain the man was dead, the boys poured salt into his wounds. When Conrad's body twitched in pain, they continued the torture. Finally, after being hit in the head with a brass eagle, the poor man stopped breathing. Relieved, the kids loaded their booty—a shotgun, VCR, camcorder, and stereo—into Conrad's van and drove away. The arresting officers were stunned by the event. "It's the worst crime scene I've ever seen," District Attorney J. Tom Morgan said.[15]

Changing Laws

In most states, all crimes committed by children under the age of sixteen were considered "delinquent acts" and as such were not punishable as crimes. As a result, children under sixteen could not be confined past the age of twenty-one, no matter what crime they had committed. The theory behind this was that children were not capable of reasoning like adults and therefore should not be punished like adults for their actions. Also, it was believed that children were more easily rehabilitated than hardened criminals.

In many cases this is true, but as the nature of juvenile crimes and the age of the perpetrators have changed, it has become apparent that we are releasing unrehabilitated, violent people on society. Twelve-year-old Billy L. is one example. While other kids his age were playing Nintendo, shooting baskets, and trading baseball cards, Billy was raping and beating homeless women in city park. Because of his age, the sentence was eighteen months in a boy's camp. After one year he was sent to a half-way house and given weekend furloughs. One weekend he simply failed to return.[16]

The case of Craig Price convinced Rhode Island that major changes were needed to their criminal statutes. In 1989, this five-foot, ten-inch, two-hundred-pound high-school football player broke into a house where Joan Heaton, a widow, and two young daughters lived. With incredible savagery, he proceeded to slaughter them, stabbing the ten-year-old sixty-two times.

After his arrest, local police reopened an unsolved murder from two years before. In that case a twenty-seven-year-old woman, Rebecca Spencer, had been stabbed fifty-eight times and left to die. Craig Price pled guilty to both crimes. But, because the crimes were committed before he was sixteen-years-old (ages fifteen and thirteen, respectively), Price could only be held until his twenty-first birthday, 11 October 1994. Rhode Island has revised their laws, but those changes can't apply in this case.[17]

Paying the Price

Cases such as these have prompted many to call for the death penalty for capital crimes committed by teens—a move unheard of in past decades. In 1988, the Supreme Court ruled that Wayne Thompson could not be executed by the state of Oklahoma for a crime he had committed when he was fifteen-years-old, which in effect set the legal age for execution at sixteen. However, at the time of Thompson's case, Oklahoma did not have a statute which set age limits for capital offenses.

In *Stanford v. Kentucky*, the Court ruled that states could execute even younger children providing they had fully examined all relevant issues and had a set age limit for the death penalty in their statutes.[18]

Prisoners of Fear

In spite of the rising statistics and increasing viciousness of juvenile violence, the majority of young people are not criminals, nor will most of them actually experience serious physical harm at the hands of their peers. But, in a sense, they are all paying a price. The age of innocence is gone. Most children no longer are free to spend the day riding their bikes around town, walk to a summer afternoon matinee, or hike to the nearby fishing hole without supervision.

Sylvester Williams, who attends Wingate High School in New York, must pass through metal detectors each morning. " 'It makes me feel safer,' says Williams. 'I don't mind, unless it makes me late for first-period class.' "[19] Other students, however, resent the measures, claiming they feel as if they are entering prison each morning.

In many neighborhoods, parents are reluctant to let their children play outside alone. A survey taken by Boston City Hospital's pediatric clinic revealed the widespread use of this protective strategy. Of the mothers questioned whose children had witnessed some violence, 85 percent said they restricted their children's outdoor activities; 57 percent of the mothers whose children had never seen violence did the same.[20]

In areas such as LA's inner city, where babies sleep in bathtubs where they won't be hit by stray bullets, or the Bronx in N.Y., where gunfire is a nightly occurrence, these precautions are prudent. But, some parents in small towns and safer suburbs are responding in the same way. Vigilance is necessary, but raising kids in a constant state of fear and paranoia is also damaging.

The scourge of violence has changed forever the way children grow up in America. Jerry Adler, a writer for *Newsweek*, observed:

Something precious has gone out of American culture, and we don't know how to get it back. We may not even realize our loss. . . . But what we've lost goes beyond the fear of crime. It is the unspoken consensus that held children to be a privileged class deserving protection from adult concerns and responsibilities.[21]

5

Life in the Hood

Robert Sandifer first came to the attention of authorities when he was twenty-two months old, after being treated for scratches and bruises on his neck, arms, and torso. The incident was reported to the state Department of Children and Family Services (DCFS) as abuse. On a cold January afternoon, just a few months later, police found him home alone with his three-and five-year-old brothers. Robert had numerous scars on his face, cordlike marks on his torso, and burns on his neck and buttocks. His siblings showed similar signs of abuse.

By the time Robert was only three, an undercurrent of rage was already apparent. When he became angry at a social worker, the toddler began swearing and grabbed a toy knife, holding the blade to her arm. The courts awarded custody of the child to his grandmother.[1]

At his grandmother's house Robert appeared to be free from the physical abuse. Deborah Dean, a neighbor from across the alley, would take the little boy to church with her family, where he sang in a children's choir with Deborah's daughter, Shavon.

But, after a while, Robert stopped attending church. With ten children of her own at home, and up to twenty other young people often sharing the three bedroom house, Robert's grandmother had little time to supervise his activities, and the child became a product of the streets. In time, he began running with a gang called the Black Disciples.

A love for cookies and other sweets earned Robert the nickname Yummy, but his method of procuring those delicacies got him banned from the neighborhood stores. A manager at the Gallery market described him as a boy who had an "11-year-old body, but he was 29 or 30 in the head. He was a slick con artist. They should have hung him in the middle of the street."[2]

Robert was brought up on charges for shoplifting at the age of eight. Two years later, a judge moved Robert to a juvenile center after hearing testimony that prostitutes were allegedly working from the grandmother's home. In spite of the placement, Robert's criminal life continued. From 1993 until his death on 28 August 1994, he appeared in court eight times for felonies, including drug possession and armed robbery. Convictions on two of those charges resulted in probation. Illinois statutes do not allow imprisonment for ten-year-olds.[3]

Like many sociopaths, Robert had never bonded with any loving adult in the early years of his life, and yet he had a disarming way of charming the adults around him. In spite of his track record, officials who worked with him could not believe he was a criminal. Many neighbors spoke of him as a menace who bullied others with guns and knives and set fires. Teachers, however, saw him as a loving, playful child.

In February of 1994, Robert ran away from the juvenile home and returned to the closest thing to a family he knew, the Black Disciples. He was picked up in June for auto theft, sentenced for thirty days, and released to his grandmother. Days later he was picked up again for burglarizing the school.

Robert's criminal activities came to a close on 28 August, however, when witnesses claim the eleven-year-old went to a local playground to take care of some gang business. Armed with a semiautomatic pistol, he began shooting at the crowd. Within minutes, Shavon Dean, his fourteen-year-old friend and neighbor, was dead.

It didn't take long for police to uncover the boy's trail. Frightened, Robert went into hiding. A neighbor who saw him shortly before his death said he appeared shaken and asked for prayer. Hours later, Robert Sandifer was found under a viaduct with two bullets in his brain. National publicity of Shavon's death had made Yummy a liability to the Black Disciples, so they executed him.[4]

History of Gangs

Gangs are not an invention of the twentieth century. In fact, they have been present in Europe and Asia for centuries. The first gangs to form in the United States—the Bowery Boys, Smith's Fly Gang, the Fly Boys, and the Long Bridge Boys—began shortly after the Revolutionary War.[5]

Without exception, the early gangs formed in poorer sections of major cities. New York City was the home of most gang activities, where membership was often based upon nationality or trade. Though most early members were not engaged in criminal activities, they were known for their fights, and would often act like unruly unions protecting their business turf from intruders. The Bowery Boys and the Five Points Gang were famous for feuding and at times would engage in such vicious fighting the army would be called in to stop them.

Early in the nineteenth century the first American criminal gangs were formed in New York. By the middle of that century, evidence of youth gangs, with members between the ages of ten and nineteen, appeared in Philadelphia. Some of these were just harmless groups of kids hanging out on street corners; others engaged in shoplifting and petty crime. The tougher, more hardened gangs were involved in violent crime and combat.[6] After the Civil War, these groups continued to slowly evolve into what we see today. It was at this time that drugs made their debut into gang culture.

In the 1920s and 1930s, Chicano gangs began to grow in Los Angeles, and by the next decade they were strongly entrenched. The fifties saw the rise of fighting gangs in New York City, Philadelphia, Boston, Chicago, Detroit, and Cleveland.[7] Rivals would engage in "rumbles" using guns, knives, and an arsenal of homemade weapons. These battles were lethal and would often result in serious injuries and death.

Because drug users were unreliable in a fight, addiction was looked down upon, and could even result in expulsion from the gang. But, slowly, drugs began to infiltrate. As the sixties came into full swing, gang activity was seldom reported, possibly due to a change of focus for the press, who now had the Vietnam War, campus riots, and terrorist attacks to occupy their attention. Nikki Cruz, a former New York City gang leader, believes that visibility decreased in part because of the increasing number of members addicted to drugs. They no longer had the time or energy for the large-scale rumbles of the past which had attracted so much attention: they were too busy finding ways to support their habits. Unfortunately, gang members still continued to die, and the shift in lifestyle made these groups prime recruiting targets for the drug lords.

Agents of the Drug Cartel

By the midseventies, gangs were back with a vengeance, but they were still confined to major cities. The majority were located in New York, Chicago, and Los Angeles, where gangs had the longest history. In 1984, Los Angeles had an estimated 450 gangs with forty thousand members, and in 1987 Chicago acknowledged 125 gangs with twelve thousand members.[8] By 1991, police estimate almost 600 teen gangs in Los Angeles with approximately seventy thousand to eighty thousand members.[9] These groups were heavily recruited by the drug cartel as a new army of retailers.

For a time, this trade was quite profitable, but as the number of drug dealers increased, the price of the goods began to drop. The most practical business solution was obvious: it was time to expand. As a result, 1986 saw an explosion of gangs nationwide as representatives of the Los Angeles gangs moved out to colonize new areas.

Girls and Gangs

Traditionally, gangs have been a male phenomenon, though there were always girls on the periphery. During the fifties that began to change as girls banded together in their own groups. They were still closely tied to the guys and would often name themselves after a "brother" gang. Though accurate numbers are not available, the New York City Youth Board estimated that there were at least six thousand female members by 1961.[10]

For most girls, the purpose of the gang was association with boys. Though often treated brutally by their "brothers," they were afforded some protection from members of rival groups. Though some female-only gangs still exist, young women are now being recruited by traditionally male gangs. In Los Angeles, girls account for approximately 15 percent of the gang population.[11] While many still participate just to be with the boys, there is an alarming trend of violence among female juveniles. "In San Antonio a 13-year-old girl allegedly beat and then held down another girl while police say several boys sexually assaulted her. In New Orleans, a 16-year-old schoolgirl pulled out a six-inch kitchen knife and plunged it into a classmates back."[12]

Federal statistics show an incredible 25.4 percent increase in violent crime by female juveniles between 1982 and 1992.[13] For some areas, the surge is even more significant. In Massachusetts, for example, 15 percent of female juvenile arrests were for violent crimes in 1987. By 1991, they account for 38 percent.[14] Karen Shonka, a deputy with the Los Angeles Sheriff's Gang Enforcement Team, says girls "are as criminal as men, but until now, they weren't considered significant. . . . They're stealing cars, selling drugs, pulling the triggers on drive-by shootings."[15]

Nineteen-year-old Regina, a member of the Playgirl Gangsters, is so adept at stealing cars she has earned the moniker (street name) of GTA, for Grand Theft Auto. But, her activities are not limited to theft. Revenge for offenses against "homegirls" is an integral part of membership. At one time, a rival gang member killed the twelve-year-old brother of a homegirl. Regina tells how she dressed as a man and set out to take care of the murderer.

> "He was after my girlfriend . . . but figured she'd suffer more if he blasted her little brothers brains." The muscles in Regina's throat tighten. "I found the guy at a back-yard beer party, bragging about the killing. I went up to him and said, 'This is the big payback from the hood.' "[16]

Regina shot the man twice in the chest. Though she aimed for his heart, he managed to survive the ordeal. "Occasionally he comes 'round looking for the guy who shot him. . . . Guess he's never gonna find him."[17]

Bloods and Crips

The Bloods (who wear red) and Crips (who wear blue), two predominately black gangs, are perhaps the most well known. These groups developed in the late 1960s in Compton, Watts, and Willowbrook in Los Angeles. Though neither side can agree on how they evolved or what started the rivalry between them, they carry a vicious antagonism toward each other. Both groups are very heavily involved in drug trafficking and as this "industry" has grown, they have absorbed many smaller gangs.

Bloods and Crips, however, do not hold monopolies on gang activity. Hispanic gangs began developing around the turn of the century, mainly to protect their neighborhoods from criminal activities from the outside. By the thirties and forties, however, they had degenerated into criminals themselves.

Skinheads, known for their racial violence, grew out of music culture of the midsixties in England, gradually finding their way into the United States. At first, these young men had long hair like the other teens from that time period, but they began to shave their heads to keep from getting their hair pulled during their frequent fights.[18]

There are actually two factions within the skinheads, the racists and nonracists. Both look alike, are violent, and are involved in serious criminal activities. The most well known are the racists, who believe in white supremacy and go by a variety of names, including Boot Boys, Hitler's Youth, and Hammer Skins. This group is not generally involved in drug trade, and their main purpose is to spread their Hitlerian doctrines and attack anyone who is not of Aryan descent.[19]

The most well known, nonracist skinhead group goes by the name SHARP, or Skinheads Against Racial Prejudice, and are just as violent as the other groups. The only difference is the object of their hatred—racist skinheads.[20]

Perhaps the most dangerous gang in America is The Posse. Originally started for the purpose of smuggling marijuana from Jamaica, they soon branched out into the cocaine market, and eventually into gun-running. Located mainly on the East Coast, this heavily armed group attracts slightly older members.[21]

Asian gangs are a unique phenomenon which has developed in this country since the migration of Vietnamese after the Vietnam War. Unlike the black and Hispanic groups, these gangs do not claim any set turf. They are involved in extortion, drugs and kidnapping, and prey mainly upon other Asians. For many members, this is a training ground for advancement into the Asian Mafia.[22]

From Wannabe to Gangbanger

There are numerous reasons kids join gangs. Part of the allure is a sense of "glamour" teens see in a dangerous, risky lifestyle. Unfortunately, the music and movie industries have helped to propagate this image. *The Warriors*, a movie about the close friendships and exciting lifestyle of New York street gangs, has been directly traced to the evolution of gangs in Chattanooga, Tennessee. The first teen gang in that city was started by a group of kids after watching the movie. In a short time, fourteen more gangs appeared, and the crime rate began to climb. In 1988, Chattanooga had its first gang-related murder.

Other reasons given for gang involvement are a desire to have friends, a need for protection, a longing for a family relationship the child does not have at home, and a desire to make money through theft or drug trade. For some, gang membership is a family tradition; for others, it's a way to deal with boredom.

Initiation into a gang, however, is brutal and sometimes deadly. The most common initiation is "jumping in," which usually involves having to fight off some or all of the members of the gang for a set period of time. This supposedly shows that the "wannabe" is willing to stick by the other members even in a fight. The same method is often employed for girl members as well, although girls joining a male gang are given another alternative. They can be "tricked in," or required to have sex with several gang members. In San Antonio, five girls walked into a clinic asking for an AIDS test after their initiation. It seems the "leader" in the gang they were joining insisted that each girl have sex with

him, even though he told them he had AIDS. The
girls all tested negative, and the consensus of opinion was that the young man had lied to test their
loyalty. What is tragic, however, is that every girl
complied.[23]

Once a girl begins this process, she is quite
often not allowed to withdraw. And, the sexual abuse
continues even after the initiation. Lana ran away
from home when she was twelve to live with J.J., her
gang-member boyfriend in a run-down, bug-infested
apartment. When J.J. insisted she have intercourse
with two of his friends, Lana complied. "I wanted
him to know that I wasn't just a kid," she explained.[24]
Another female member commented, "Mostly guys
get the girls drunk while we're partying and then a
bunch of them have sex with one girl. That's just
the way life is around here."[25] Though girls often
join the group for acceptance and affection, they
usually end up alone, on welfare, raising children.

In some gangs, however, initiations are taking
on a more deadly tone, with initiates being asked to
commit theft, rape, and even murder. Sometimes
the target is a rival member; often it is an innocent
bystander. An incident in the Cherry Creek area of
Denver is a good example. It was late when Mary
(not her real name) stopped for gas. Fortunately,
she had gone to a station which required prepay-
ments. Mary walked inside, paid for the gas, and
went back to the car. But the pump wasn't turned
on. She looked up toward the station attendant,
who was watching her while he talked on the phone.
With growing frustration, she motioned at the pump,
but the attendant didn't budge. Finally, she stormed
back into the station to demand that the pump be
turned on, only to discover that the attendant's quick
thinking had saved her life. From the corner of his

eye he had seen someone sneak into the back seat of the car and lie down. Instead of flipping the appropriate switch, he called the police. The intruder was apprehended and finally confessed he was undergoing a gang initiation that required him to rape and murder a woman from a wealthy part of town.

Violence: A Way of Life

Though gangs still account for a small percentage of our nation's crime, the rapid growth and random viciousness of acts committed by young people make gang violence a special concern. Robbery, extortion, drug trafficking, and theft are considered occupations. Other crimes include rape, assault, arson, kidnapping, and murder. Los Angeles, which is plagued with the greatest number of gang members, reports almost one gang-related murder a day. Drive-by shootings are a popular way of terrorizing rivals, seeking revenge, and are sometimes a method of initiation. In 1991, the LA police recorded 1,548 gang-related drive-by shootings, with at least 2,222 people being shot at.[26] In some large cities, gangs account for 30 percent of the murders.[27]

Most of the violence is related to turf violations and imagined insults. A sheriff's deputy from Los Angeles reported to the *Wall Street Journal*, "The reasons these groups shoot each other is so stupid you wouldn't believe it. Throwing up your gang's sign in rival turf is a killing offense. Life is cheaper than cheap."[28]

Quite often those hit in drive-bys are innocent victims, yet the shooters show little remorse. When an eleven-year-old boy was shot to death in Los Angeles, the killer told police, "The child shouldn't

have been there. I was aiming for someone else."
Another gang member described shooting a rival
and his family for walking on the wrong turf.

> I strapped it [an AK-47] to the seat . . . and
> we circled around and pulled up on this [guy]
> from two blocks away, crept up on him slow
> like, and I just gave it to him . . . I lit his —
> — up! I killed him—shot his baby in the
> leg—crippled his wife! . . . She's in a wheel-
> chair now, I heard, wearin' a voicebox, 'cause
> one of the bullets caught her in the throat.[29]

Another fad among gang members is to rob
other young people for shoes, clothes, and jewelry.
Chicago police report over sixty incidents a month
involving jackets and shoes. Others seem to need
no provocation at all to kill. According to Steve
Collura, a former New York police detective, "These
guys today, they're cold-blooded killers. Kill you for
a shirt, a piece of chicken, a dirty look."[30]

Lost Kids

Not every gang member is a hardened, blood-
thirsty psychopath, however. Many kids just seem to
get caught up in a situation that can explode out of
control. In some neighborhoods, membership is a
prerequisite for a social life. Most young people
who join gangs come from homes without fathers
or any significant male role models to enforce discipline. Many kids are from abusive situations and
are looking for the affection and sense of belonging
they don't get at home. Some of the kids are homeless, either runaways or children abandoned by families who do not want them or cannot deal with the
responsibilities. These kids are easily drawn into a
group that will offer them food, shelter, and a sense

of belonging. And, life in a gang, no matter how violent, appears safer than life on the streets.

When Baby J. was ten years old, her father, a gang member, was sent to prison for dealing drugs. Left in the projects with a crack-addicted mother, Baby J. started selling drugs to help support the family. At eleven, she became a member of the Grape Street Watts Crips. Three years later, after several arrests, she was placed in a foster home with a firm but loving caretaker. As her self-esteem rose, Baby J. decided to leave the gang. What she had needed was love and guidance, something the gang could not supply. "Most homies will tell you in private they wish they could get out, and what they really want is just to be wanted, noticed and loved by their parents."[31]

Matt (real name not used) grew up in an abusive home. His father was gone, and his mother changed boyfriends frequently. Looking for a sense of escape, he joined up with a gang. One evening, after getting drunk, the young teen jumped into a car with a friend and drove down the street shooting at parked cars. As the boys rounded the corner, Matt shot at another vehicle—only this one wasn't empty. A family was just returning home, and the six-year-old boy, still strapped in his seatbelt, took a bullet in the neck. Paramedics arriving on the scene were able to keep the boy alive, but the vertebrae in his neck were shattered. He will spend the rest of his life in a wheelchair hooked to a breathing machine.

At the sentencing hearing, the crippled child looked up at the judge and said in a rasping voice, "I want Matt to go to jail." "I know, honey, he will," the judge replied. Obviously, shaken, Matt could not look at his victim. With trembling hands, he

read an apology to the family and a poem he had
written, which ended with the lines,

> When I pulled the trigger that day
> I took two lives.
> For neither one of us will ever
> walk free in the sun.

6

Life Is Cheap

"Human life means nothing," Derrick O'Brien bragged on a Houston television show. The next night he made his point. Returning home from a pool party, two young girls cut through a wooded area and encountered Derrick and five fellow gang members. "Let's get 'em," one boy said, and a vicious, barbaric attack ensued. The girls were beaten, repeatedly raped, and strangled with a belt and shoelaces. To make certain their victims were dead, the boys stomped on their necks.[1]

This brutal, senseless crime shocked Houston, as did the calloused attitudes of the six suspects, whose ages ranged form fourteen to seventeen. Upon hearing of the impending murder charges, Omar Villareal, seventeen, reportedly gloated, "Hey, great! We've hit the big time."[2]

As juvenile offenders become younger and their crimes ever more vicious, it has become apparent that we are raising children who place no value on life. But, in a society that no longer considers life to be sacred, this phenomenon should not be surprising. We have devalued human life, and this is a natural consequence.

No Longer Sacred

Appalled by the centuries of practices of abortion, infanticide, and euthanasia, Hippocrates established the famous Hippocratic Oath that required physicians to use their skills only for healing. His students were forbidden to perform abortions or in any way hasten death, even at the request of the patient. Hippocrates' influence was so profound that for over two thousand years doctors have sworn to uphold this oath. Recently, however, many within the medical profession have veered drastically from its creed.

The shift began slowly at first in the philosophical arena with German philosopher George Hegel, whose ideas became very popular in universities in the nineteenth and early twentieth centuries. Hegel denied the existence of any moral authority. "God is God only in so far as he knows himself," he argued. In a social sense, man owed strict allegiance to the state, not to a divine being.

Hegel's teachings were very popular on university campuses and became the justification for the mass murder of millions under Hitler. Hegel's disciples "taught that it was impossible to know truth and that moral absolutes could not exist. Everything that exists, according to Hegel, is in a process of change. No one can know God or truly discern whether something is right or wrong. It depends upon the circumstance."[3]

The influence of Hegel's situational ethics was very apparent in a short book published in 1920 by Alfred Hoche, a prominent psychiatrist, and Karl Binding, a renowned jurist. *Releasing Persons from Lives Devoid of Value* brought the topic of euthanasia to the forefront. Hoche and Binding recommended killing worthless persons, such as mental patients and those who are chronically ill. They insisted that doctors had a duty to grant such unfortunate people "Death with Dignity," and to save financial resources being wasted on those who had nothing to offer the state.

Hoche introduced the idea of "mental death" and applied it to the retarded or brain damaged. "He described these people as human ballast and recommended that killing them would be an allowable, useful act. He maintained these people were already dead. The doctor's duty was to simply complete the death process by killing the body."[4]

This book completely undermined the Judeo-Christian ethic of the sanctity of life.

> Soon afterwards, in 1921, 1922, and 1923, wounded German World War I veterans who obstinately refused to die were the first to be put to death by euthanasia. As the decade wore on, the practice was extended to other invalids, the handicapped, and the mentally retarded.[5]

These practices had so seared the conscience of the medical and academic communities that there was little opposition when Hitler issued the first direct order for euthanasia on 1 September 1939, targeting patients in state institutions "who had been ill for five years or more or who were unable to work." Information collected from questionnaires was given to university psychologists who never saw the patients. They were then entrusted with the responsibility of determining who would die.[6]

Dr. Leo Alexander, consultant to the office of the Chief of Counsel for War Crimes, had access to many Nazi records, including a report by a member of the Frankfurt-am-Main court of appeals. This document confirmed that the Holocaust began with the elimination of the old, the mentally impaired, the chronically ill, and people suffering from multiple sclerosis, Parkinson's Disease, and brain tumors.[7] If the old and infirm were to be done away with, then it seemed only natural for deformed or handicapped infants and children to suffer the same fate. In fact, Germany's first gas chambers were not at the death camps; they were in hospitals, operated by doctors.

Sanctity of Life in America

The United States was founded by people who believed in God, absolute values, and the sanctity of human life. These convictions were clearly defined in the Declaration of Independence. "We hold these truths to be self-evident, that all men are created equal, that they are endowed by their Creator with certain inalienable Rights that among these are Life, Liberty, and the pursuit of Happiness." An adherence to these truths is vital to any free government. All other rights and freedoms are derived from a belief in the uniqueness and sanctity of human life. Whenever these values have been abandoned, anarchy or tyranny has ensued.

Yet, the battle to destroy this foundation in America has been going on for nearly a century. John Dewey, the Father of Progressive Education, sought to expel any concept of God and values from the educational system. Margaret Sanger, an outspoken atheist and socialist, became influential in destroying the concept of the sanctity of human life. Sanger founded the Voluntary Parenthood League in 1914 and opened the first birth control clinic in the United States in New York. A radical feminist, Sanger deplored the institution of marriage, calling it "the most degenerating influence in the social order." On another occasion she wrote, "The most merciful thing that the large family does to one of its infant members is to kill it."[8]

Sanger became enamored with the idea of eugenics, or selective breeding of humans, a concept adopted by the Nazis. Like the Nazis, she believed that Jews, blacks, and Hispanics were inferior and should be weeded out. She even published an article on selective sterilization by Dr. Ernest Rubin, Hitler's director of genetic sterilization. Not surprisingly, Planned Parenthood is proud to call Margaret Sanger their founder.

Changing Values

Gradually, public opinion on life-related issues began to change. These changes were slow at first, but have accelerated greatly, especially after the introduction of the "Values Clarification" curriculum into schools. Students were given hypothetical life and death situations, required to debate the "value" of their classmates or parents, and chose who should live or die. The purpose of these exercises was to eradicate the idea that all human life was sacred. They taught that life was *not* an inalienable right; that society had the right to determine whether or not a person deserves to live. As these philosophies took hold in the universities, the debate over abortion and euthanasia heated up.

Death for Convenience

In 1859, the American Medical Association (AMA) passed a resolution condemning abortions and urging state legislatures to make the practice illegal. Their efforts were effective, and before long abortion was a major crime in every state. A century later, however, the prevailing mood of doctors had changed, and the AMA became a leader in the move to repeal abortion laws.[9] Changing public opinion required changing public perception, and the dehumanizing of the unborn began. The unborn child was not a baby; it was an embryo, fetus, or mass of tissue. Instead, attention was focused on the "rights" of the woman seeking to rid herself of an inconvenience.

In 1957, the American Law Institute responded to these shifting values by asking state legislatures to liberalize existing statutes. The suggestions were not accepted immediately, but by the 1960s, laws began to change.[10] Each state still had the power to restrict or forbid this procedure, however, until 1973 when the Supreme Court ruled in *Roe v. Wade* that an unborn baby had no rights and that women should be able to have an abortion for any reason. State statutes which were more restrictive than the *Roe v. Wade* guidelines became null and void.

Since that landmark case the number of abortions has skyrocketed. In America, one-third of all pregnancies each year are deliberately terminated. An average of 4,320 babies die per day at the hands of abortionists. "That means that every twenty seconds, one baby dies; every minute, three die; every hour, 180 die; every week, 30,240 die; every month, 129,600 die. Every year, 1,576,000 unborn children" are legally slaughtered.[11]

Abortion, the ending of human life, has become more than just a difficult decision made after much deliberation by a woman in unfortunate circumstances. It is a multibillion dollar industry. In addition to the fees charged for performing the operation, the dead babies themselves have become a profitable commodity. The fetal tissue industry is booming since President Clinton gave official sanction to fetal tissue research. According to Dr. Curt Harris, an endocrinologist and bioethicist, this has the potential of becoming a $6 billion-a-year business.[12]

A New Kind of Harvest

The "harvesting" and sale of fetal organs is another lucrative source of revenue. The concept of organ donations from babies who have died of natural causes or accidental deaths is admirable. Though nothing can eliminate the grief of parents who have lost a child, there is a sense of comfort in knowing that you have helped to save another life. But, to allow abortionists to profit from killing is unconscionable.

In another disturbing move, permission is now being sought to "harvest" vital organs from some infants while they are still alive. Loma Linda University Medical Center performed experiments on anencephalic infants, removing their organs for transplant *before* death. Anencephalic babies are born without the top of their skull or the cerebral cortex. These tragic children live for only a few days and never experience consciousness, yet they *are* alive.

In 1988, when prolife activists discovered that these children were being murdered for their organs, the experiments were shut down. In an effort to get around the protests, "legislators and medical personnel attempted to have the definition of brain death changed to include live anencephalic infants. They were to be considered dead under a newly created category called 'respiratory brain death.' "[13]

Loma Linda failed in their attempt to expand the definition of death, but the battle is not over. In early 1995, the Council of Ethics and Judicial Affairs of the AMA announced that they found no ethical or moral problems with harvesting organs from living anencephalic infants. The justification for this position, the council stated, was the fact that these children do not experience consciousness, so they should not be considered alive. AMA leadership has asked the committee to reconsider its position, but they do not have the authority to override the council's position.[14]

If the AMA succeeds in their move to change existing laws to kill living babies for their organs, then it only seems logical that it will become easier to justify taking organs from others who are unconscious, or whose mental capabilities do not meet an acceptable standard.

Selective Destruction

During the Nazi regime, handicapped children were viewed as a subspecies not worthy of continued existence. They were of no utilitarian purpose to the state or to themselves. In fact, it was reasoned, a physician who rescued a person from such a worthless and unfulfilling existence was committing a humanitarian act. "Defective" infants were quickly dispatched. In America, we have chosen to follow this example.

Advanced medical technology has enabled doctors to diagnose certain mental and physical disabilities prior to birth and thereby enable parents to abort a "defective fetus." The child's right to live is not seen as inalienable. Many professionals argue that it is morally and fiscally irresponsible to allow such a child to consume our valuable resources. Others actually see ending this life as a humanitarian act. Thomas and Celia Scully wrote in *Playing God*:

> In considering whether or not to treat a new-
> born, most experts believe that the *primary*
> issue is what's in the child's best interests. If
> his mental and physical handicaps are over-
> whelming and it would be inhumane to pro-
> long his life, then treatment should be with-
> held or withdrawn. After all, saving an in-
> fant for a life of suffering is hardly a hu-
> mane and loving act.[15]

Increasing numbers of handicapped babies are
being denied medical treatment and food to ensure
their death. Some infants are born with duodenal
atresia, or blocked intestines, a condition which can
be completely corrected with surgery. If the child is
"normal," then doctors perform surgery. Under
those circumstances, the courts would not allow
parents to forbid the life-saving treatment. Any
parent who would attempt to interfere would be
charged with child abuse.

However, if the newborn in question has Down's
syndrome, a condition which causes mild retardation, then the parents and physician may opt to
withhold treatment and let the baby starve to death.
Though it is technically illegal to starve children
simply because they have Downs Syndrome, that is
exactly what is happening. The child is being murdered because of his mental state. Dr. Anthony Shaw
describes watching an infant die in this manner.

> When surgery is denied [the doctor] must
> try to keep the infant from suffering while
> natural forces sap the baby's life away. As a
> surgeon whose natural inclination is to use
> the scalpel to fight off death, standing by
> and watching a salvageable baby die is the
> most emotionally exhausting experience I
> know. It is easy at a conference, in a theo-

retical discussion, to decide that such infants should be allowed to die. It is altogether different to stand by in the nursery and watch as dehydration and infection wither a tiny being over hours and days. This is a terrible ordeal for me and the hospital staff—much more than for the parents who never set foot in the nursery.[16]

What is appalling is that Doctor Shaw supports the decision to let handicapped children with this condition die. He just regrets that there isn't a more humane way of disposing of the child.

Infanticide

Other doctors have become more outspoken in advocating active euthanasia for handicapped babies. Like their predecessors in Germany, they do not deem such babies worthy of life and view their destruction as humane. Earl Shelp, an assistant professor of medical ethics at Baylor College in Waco, Texas, asserts that active euthanasia (the intentional killing of a person through lethal injection or some other means) is appropriate for infants and in many cases is the best option.[17] Raymond Duff and A.G.M. Campbell are neonatologists who agree that laws should be changed to permit the killing of "selected newborns as a means of liberating the infant from pointless, dehumanizing treatment."[18]

H. Tristan Engelhardt, Jr., summed up this position in "The Foundation of Bioethics":

What is wrong in murder is not the taking of a person's life, but that it is taken without that individual's permission and in addition in many circumstances that it is a maleficent act. Infants are not persons whose autonomy can be violated or entities who can suffer

through having their goals thwarted. A pain-
less death through active euthanasia may
offer less suffering than passive euthanasia,
and at times less pain than life itself.[19]

Duty to Die, Duty to Kill

In 1982, Gov. Richard Lamm of Colorado caused
a stir when he stated in a public speech that the
elderly had a "duty to die" and get out of the way,
like leaves falling off a tree and fertilizing the ground
for other plants to grow. He denounced the amount
of money spent on medical costs for people who
had passed their most productive years.

Howard Caplan, a geriatrics doctor who operates three nursing homes in Los Angeles, goes one
step further asserting that a doctor should have the
right to actively end the life of patients who are
comatose, terminally ill, or who are "no longer able
to live active, meaningful lives."[20] Helga Kuhse, director of the Centre for Human Bioethics at Monash
University in Australia is another strong proponent
of murdering patients. "I believe there will be times
when it is better that a patient be killed rather than
allowed to die—either because the process of dying
involves much unnecessary suffering or because a
competent patient asks her doctor for help in dying."[21]

Unfortunately, there are many within the medical profession who believe doctors actually have a
duty to kill. Dr. Timothy Johnson, medical editor
for "ABC News" and an ordained minister in the
Evangelical Covenant Church has stated: "I personally believe that helping someone die in peace and
without pain, even if it might hasten the biological
timetable of death by a few hours or even days, is
not only acceptable but is mandatory for modern

medical care."[22] While he personally only advocates passive euthanasia, or the withdrawing of life support, he insists that it would be wrong to condemn another doctor who actively assists a terminal patient's death. While opposing legalizing physician-assisted suicide, he points to Holland as an appropriate model of social compromise. There, euthanasia is still illegal, but the government has agreed not to prosecute any physician who kills patients as long as certain guidelines have been met.

Others, like bioethicist Peter Singer, are less squeamish about ending human life. He insists that there is nothing unique about people and that defective infants should be destroyed the same way that a defective animal would be. In fact, he argues, in many cases animals are of more use than humans.

> If we compare a severely defective human infant with a nonhuman animal, a dog or a pig, for example, we will often find the nonhuman to have superior capacities. . . . Only the fact that the defective infant is a member of the species, *Homo Sapiens*, leads it to be treated differently from the dog or pig. Species membership alone, however, is not morally relevant.[23]

Unfortunately, this philosophy has been adopted by many in the medical profession, as one Washington couple discovered. Their infant son was born gravely ill, and surgery was indicated to make certain the child would live. But, when the parents requested the surgery, the physician and hospital refused. The baby was severely retarded, the parents were told, and should be left to die. The parents demanded the surgery be done and threatened to move their son to another hospital if necessary. In a disturbing twist, the hospital actually filed child abuse charges against the parents for refusing to kill their child! Through emergency court proceedings, the parents were able to transfer their baby to a more congenial hospital. The little boy responded quickly to medication, and surgery was no longer necessary. The new physicians also insist that any retardation which may exist is not as severe as originally diagnosed.

Public Response

The extent to which public opinion has been swayed by this debate can be seen in the progress of legislation allowing physician-assisted suicide. In 1991 and 1992, Washington and California narrowly defeated proposals which would have allowed doctors to prescribe lethal doses of medication to terminal patients. In 1994, the Hemlock Society's home state of Oregon became the first to pass such legislation.

Under the Oregon Death with Dignity Act, a patient with six months or less to live could be given fatal prescriptions. Proponents praised the measure, claiming it would reduce the horrendous cost of caring for terminally ill patients. The measure, which will be tied up in the courts for some time, was supported by the Washington State Democratic Party, the National Organization for Women, and the ACLU.[24]

The Road to Holocaust?

Proponents of abortion and euthanasia scoff at the idea that such measures violate human dignity or that they will lead down a "slippery slope" to holocaust. This is nonsense, they claim, and point to Holland as proof. But, the situation in Holland is exactly what the United States should avoid.

In 1990, the Dutch government set up a committee to investigate the practice of euthanasia. Their findings revealed just how far down the slope that country had gone. Doctors are not only killing terminal patients who have requested assistance or comatose patients whose families have made the decision: according to the study, "14,691 people died in 1990 by involuntary euthanasia, which means that these lives were cut short by doctors without the request, consent or knowledge of the patients." In 45 percent of the cases which occurred in a hospital, the murder was carried out without the knowledge or consent of the patient or his family. According to the report, 1,474 of these victims were fully conscious and competent at the time a doctor arbitrarily, and without their consent, decided to put them to death.[25]

Deadly Inconsistencies

If many young people in America today show a brazen disrespect for life, it is because we as a society no longer view life as sacred. We punish kids for crimes that "professionals" are allowed to commit. For example, if a pregnant teen is caught using drugs, she is charged with child abuse and child endangerment. If the child subsequently dies after birth because of the mother's behavior during pregnancy, she can be charged with the baby's death. However, if that same pregnant teen chooses to abort her baby, then all child abuse charges are dropped, the abortionist is paid, and the young woman is praised for acting responsibly and compassionately toward the infant.

Again, when a young girl gives birth to an unwanted baby and abandons it to die in a trash dumpster, she is charged with murder. However, if she chooses to go to an abortionist at any point prior to labor, the doctor can kill the baby. One danger of waiting that long to abort has always been the possibility that the child might be born alive. But, abortionists are now allowed to use a new procedure guaranteed to kill the child. He may deliver the baby feet first, stopping it before the head comes out. Then scissors are jammed into the baby's skull and the brains are suctioned out. Under these brutal conditions, no one is charged with murder. And, when babies with Down's syndrome are born needing extra medical attention, society is allowed to starve them to death.

So, does society's lack of regard for human life have an impact on our youth? Some teen-agers believe it does. After an eighteen-year-old senior was murdered at school, the Norland Senior High newspaper sponsored an essay contest to help students deal with the tragedy. The winning entry, by freshman Wilkie Ferguson, made the following observation:

> "I believe that the school is a product of its surrounding community and that violence in school won't stop until community violence stops," Ferguson wrote. "The people who commit these crimes have a lack of respect for life; their own and others. This respect must be instilled in everyone before any forward steps can be made."[26]

But, society cannot teach what it does not believe. We cannot expect our youth to respect human life until we as a society restore the belief that *all* human life is sacred.

7

The Role of the Schools

Abraham Lincoln once observed that the philosophy of the schools of one generation would become the philosophy of the government in the next generation. The truth of this statement has been evident throughout history. The power of schools can be—and has been—used for much good. The main purpose of public school should be to teach basic academic studies and to ensure that graduates have the necessary skills to compete in industry and become self-supporting.

But, this cannot be done in a moral vacuum. Children spend almost as much time at school as they do at home, which places certain obligations upon teachers. Our public educators should respect the rights of parents and refrain from using the classroom as a campaign platform. They should also promote values such as honesty, loyalty, industry, goal-setting, achievement skills, accountability, and self-government; all qualities needed to live successfully in society.

Indoctrination vs. Education

But, too many times schools have been used as indoctrination centers to shape the minds and attitudes of the young in an effort to make major shifts in societal values. Perhaps the most graphic example of this comes from Nazi Germany. Hitler did not just suddenly appear upon the scene and persuade adults to forsake their conscience and commit unspeakable atrocities. The indoctrination of Nazi philosophy throughout German society had been gaining momentum since the party's origin in 1919. Hitler Youth meetings were held on Sunday mornings, which conveniently interfered with church services. Attendance was ostensibly voluntary; however, as the party gained influence, many reluctant children were escorted at gunpoint to these sessions.

Powerful as it was, a once-a-week class could never have accomplished such a major shift in values if it had not been for the participation of the public schools. The Nazi party, which had grown slowly at first, gained incredible momentum after the worldwide financial crisis of 1929. As the party's influence increased, it had a significant impact upon education. Robert Edwin Herzstein, a professor of European history, describes the importance of the classroom to the party.

> Public education in the Third Reich quickly became a weapon in the campaign of hate. Every school teacher in Germany was forced to become a member of the National Socialist Teachers' League and to swear an oath of loyalty to Hitler. Courses in "racial sciences" were introduced into the curricula, and textbooks were hastily produced to lend to Nazi ideology a scholarly legitimacy.[1]

Economic woes following World War I had virtually destroyed the German middle class. The public was eager to find a scapegoat and cling to a leader who promised change. As a result, little was said as the vilification of the Jewish race and democratic ideals invaded the press, theater, workplace, and schools. The Nazi party's official daily newspaper, the *Voikischer Reobachter*, became required reading in current-events classes. Politically correct children's books portrayed Germans as "strong, blond and happy" and Jews as "bloated, swarthy and malevolent, 'the greatest scoundrels in the whole Reich,' as one of the books put it."[2] Illustrations from primary readers showed revolting "Jewish" child molesters offering unsuspecting German children candy. Posters showing correct Aryan features and distorted Jewish profiles were hung around the classroom. Children whose features most exemplified the correct Nordic features were often singled out for praise.[3]

Shifting Role of American Schools

Traditionally, most American children were educated at home or in private schools. Those public schools which did exist were under strict community control—without state or federal interference. These methods were highly successful, and the nation boasted a 99 percent literacy rate in the early 1880s.[4] At least ten U.S. presidents and numerous other significant figures in history were products of home-schooling. State involvement in public education first appeared in Massachusetts in the late 1840s, though actual control was still local. Parents were allowed to choose the form of education they desired and remained the primary dictators of course content and values.[5]

It was not until the early 1900s that compulsory attendance laws were passed throughout the country and tax-supported, public schools became the primary mode of education. At this time, the theories and reforms of John Dewey, an American philosopher and educator, were gaining popularity. A "scientific humanist," and an original signer of the *Humanist Manifesto*, Dewey detested religion and believed that society had evolved beyond the need of a God. Man should only believe in that which he could experience.[6]

While teaching at the University of Chicago from 1894 to 1904, Dewey became very interested in educational theory and reform. A self-proclaimed "democratic socialist," those reforms reflected his very liberal views. He decried authoritarian methods and denounced the prevailing emphasis of schools on the study of history and the classics. History should only be taught to the extent that it would serve some purpose in the present or future.

Dewey was given an opportunity to put his theories into practice at an experimental laboratory school, referred to as the Dewey School. Formal curricula were replaced with more hands-on, experience-based activities. Rote learning was thrown out, and phonics was replaced with the "look-say" method of sight reading, a program developed earlier for the deaf but abandoned as ineffective.

These innovative—albeit, inferior—experiments were enthusiastically received by many educators and earned Dewey the title of Father of Progressive Education. Though many of Dewey's followers carried his theories much further than he had intended, he was still responsible for bringing secular humanism into America's public school system.

The NEA

John Dewey found much support in the leadership of the National Education Association (NEA). Founded in 1857 as the National Teacher's Association, its intent was to promote professionalism and high standards among teachers. During the early years, the association viewed itself as a professional organization, strongly opposing strikes and other methods used by most labor unions. However, as the NEA began to adopt Dewey's theories, it's leadership became more radical and dictatorial.

As early as 1934, the NEA made its desire for absolute control over education clear in the Report of the Committee on Resolutions on the NEA, which states:

> The National Education Association *unqualifiedly* endorses the principle that *all* school affairs, including budgets and the appointments of teachers and officials, should be under the management of school authorities without interference from political or other special groups [i.e., parents] (emphasis in original).[7]

In order to mitigate parental and community involvement, the NEA consistently pushed for more federal funding, larger school districts, and NEA oversight over all community input. Claiming that states have a "compelling interest" in the education of our children, since they will be the contributing citizens of tomorrow, the NEA has been a driving force to have the school replace the family in guiding the education and values of children.

In the early 1960s, the NEA ceased being a professional organization with voluntary membership. To increase its power and funding base, it requested and was granted status as a labor union. With this designation, teachers working in states without Right to Work laws were forced to join the NEA or lose their jobs. This placed a large number of teachers in the difficult position of being forced to provide financial support to a lobbying organization with views abhorrent to their own, or leaving their chosen professions.

In spite of the obvious directive for unions to watch out for the interests of all their members, the NEA is quite open in their bias toward teachers who agree with their agenda, as evidenced at the NEA Annual Convention in 1970 when then-union president George Fishers "proclaimed that the union intends to control 'who enters, who stays, and who leaves the profession. Once this is done we can also control the teacher training institutions.' "[8]

Yet, this organization, which was founded to promote excellence in the teaching profession, consistently objects to any measure that would bring more discipline to the classroom or require a measured level of competency from its members. Teachers demand, and rightly so, to be considered professionals. However, their union is not willing to allow them to function as such. In every other professional field, a person is judged by ability to perform and results achieved. Yet, the NEA opposes advancement on merit and competency testing for teachers.

Agents of Social Change

There has been a disturbing trend of educators who see themselves as agents of social change, usurping roles once reserved for parents. John Boyles, editor of *Educator's Newsletter*, wrote:

The day is fast approaching when the schools

will be acknowledged for what they are becoming: society's agreed-upon vehicle for
instituting social change.

There appears to be no alternative to acknowledging that we have created a way of
living in which public employees will perform a significant fraction of functions traditionally left to families.

Marx and other theoreticians of social
changes—Lenin, Gandhi, and Mao Tse Tung—
have all spoken of the necessity of destroying the traditional fabric of family life in
order to accommodate the needs of society
undergoing economic transformation.[9]

School vs. Parent

As the NEA has successfully campaigned for
increased governmental control over education, the
rights of parents in these matters has significantly
decreased. (Coincidentally, the literacy rate has
dropped as government control of schools has increased.) Parents no longer have much influence
over curriculum. When they object to occultic or
sexually explicit literature in the school libraries,
they are castigated as "right-wing, fundamentalist
book-burners." The schools self-righteously insist
upon the students' "right" to access to such material. Yet, this same "right" does not apply to the
Bible or materials which promote Judeo-Christian
ethics, topics the NEA has deemed to be offensive.

The situation has escalated to the point that
school's now operate under the doctrine on *in loco
parentis,* which allows the state to take the place of
the parent. When a prosecuting attorney in Colorado was questioned over the current practice of

allowing social workers to come into schools, inter-
rogate students, conduct strip searches, and actually
abduct children from school without parental notification, he replied that the authority came from
this legal doctrine. Because of this doctrine, when a
child is enrolled in, dropped off at, or attends class
in a public school, *he becomes the property of the state.*

Today the NEA operates as the largest professional organization in the world. With its headquar-
ters in Washington, D.C., it has become a powerful
force in dictating the direction of modern education. The NEA provides legislative consultation to
local, state, and federal governments, directs curriculum, provides legal and defense assistance, and
makes political endorsements. In recent years, it
has consistently instructed its members to vote for
liberal candidates and campaigns strongly for legislation which would grant special rights based on
sexual orientation, abortion on demand, and elimination of parental notification of abortions performed on minors. The NEA is also a strong sup-
porter of Outcome Based Education (OBE), early
sex education, school-based health clinics which
provide abortion counseling, and school sponsored
condom distribution. Not surprisingly, the NEA is
in favor of ratifying the United Nations Convention
on the Rights of the Child.

The NEA has also been outspoken about its
intent that the schools replace the parent in teaching values to the students. When the NEA began
promoting Values Clarification curriculum to its
membership, they released a document titled "Values and Valuing—Parents and Students," which presented traditional values as an outmoded remnant
of " 'good old days' as a time when our country was
largely agricultural." The NEA warned that some

parents may object to values education since it would lead "young people to explore and analyze, rather than accept, the traditional values of our society." The document went on to explain that " 'Young people grow up in a much more complex world,' and consequently would be better off to abandon traditional values and 'establish modes of alternative problem-solving for the future.' "[10]

But, it isn't just the idea of young people analyzing values that was so objectionable—this is a necessary part of personal development. The problems with values clarification were twofold: first, it sought to undermine an area rightly reserved for the parents; and second, these are not neutral exercises at all, but a blatant attempt to reshape the values of a generation. Exercises included placing children in traumatic scenarios and forcing them to make ridiculous decisions no child should face. For example, in one exercise, children were told to pretend that they were in a nuclear war. At the prompting of their teachers, they hid under their desks and pretended it was a cave big enough to hold themselves and their parents. Then the children were given the "values" dilemma: there was only enough food for two. In order for anyone to survive, the third would have to be sent out into the nuclear fallout to die. The child was to decide which parent should die and state their reasons.

Various versions of this scenario abounded; some required the teacher to divide the class into small groups for peer evaluation. One such popular exercise required students to pretend they had been shipwrecked and were in a lifeboat. The boat was not big enough to hold all of the survivors, so one person was to be chosen to die to save the others. The classmates were to discuss the various attributes of each person in the group and then vote on who would be cast out to die. The damage done to students who endured these outrageous programs was significant—especially those students not deemed worthy to live by their classmates.

But, the underlying purpose for such insane activities was an attack against the belief that all human life has intrinsic value—a belief not shared by the pro-abortion NEA. A person's right to live was seen as subjective, based upon the opinions of others and what contributions that person was likely to make to society. Is it any wonder that "quality of life" and "personal choice" have been accepted as legitimate guidelines for determining whether a person shall live or die? This type of teaching in the schools played a significant role in legalizing abortion upon demand and in helping to pass the first physician-assisted suicide measure in America.

Though the scenarios and methods have changed from time to time, the schools are still very much involved in this devaluing process. History books have been rewritten to exclude an "offensive" mention to the religious, Judeo-Christian heritage of this country. Absolute values have been shelved for situational ethics. At many grammar schools, students are not even taught the Pledge of Allegiance. When parents wish to sit in on sex-ed or self-esteem classes, they are denied that right. "The presence of a parent can be very stifling and uncomfortable for a child," one teacher explained to a concerned parent who wished to sit in on a self-esteem course her daughter had been asked to attend. "We want her to feel free to discuss anything on her mind, including her home life. Your presence might stifle that discussion." Another teacher encouraged her students to create a bulletin board around the theme "I disagree with my parents about . . ."

Fighting Back

One method parents still have of exerting some influence over public education is through local school boards, but those who attempt to do so should be prepared for strong resistance. That is precisely what candidates for the Littleton (Colo.) School Board discovered. In 1993, Colorado passed HB1313 which mandated Outcome Based Education state-wide. This bill was an NEA dream, requiring educational "professionals" to set performance standards for high school graduation, with no provision for parental or tax-payer input. The measure, of course, could only be enforced by the counties, and several counties were quick to respond. Aurora designed a measure that would deny graduation based upon credit units taken and grade point average alone. Course selection was also to be altered, and one draft showed "English being replaced by communication, U.S. History by multicultural studies and physical education by 'life/career management.' "[11] Another Colorado county had included thirty hours of mandated community service and the nebulous requirement that graduates demonstrate that they were "complex thinkers and ethical people."[12]

The Littleton (Colo.) School Board, already a strong proponent of such legislation, quickly formulated similar standards. Students would no longer be required to complete a given number of units in English, math, science, etc. Grades and tests were downplayed, while portfolios of students' compositions and artwork received more emphasis. Students would be required to show that they could write a letter (something which should have been taught in grammar school), perform basic math computations, and demonstrate before a committee, proficiency in human relations and personal growth. What alarmed many parents was the lack of quantitative evaluation for such criteria.

A review of sample questions to be used by the graduation evaluation boards only intensified that concern. The questions were designed in such a way that "A" students could be denied diplomas if they were unwilling to give "politically correct" answers to many subjective questions. Conversely, students who were barely proficient in academics could still bluff their way into graduation. But, most ominous was the requirement that each student prepare a personal mental health plan which met with the committee's approval.

In the fall of 1993, three of the five Littleton School Board seats went up for grabs, a bipartisan trio joined together to run under a back-to-basics platform. They promised to throw out the OBE reforms and place renewed emphasis upon learning basic math, science, and English skills. Candidates from other counties in the state followed suit. This raised the ire of the NEA, which pumped sixty thousand dollars in the Jefferson County race alone, which included

> [mailing] brochures accusing three conservative candidates of being religious fundamentalists who want to destroy public schools. The brochure, complete with red headlines, outraged the candidates who were accused and raised eyebrows even among some voters who usually make common cause with the union on education and funding issues.[13]

Knowing that the charge of Religious Right or right-wing fundamentalist is an effective way to smear a candidate, OBE supporters in Littleton adopted this tactic as well. Attendees at a planning meeting for "reform" (OBE) candidates revealed that the

" 'reform' backers decided to level the charge of 'religious right' " because "the community could not tolerate that."[14] For the record, none of the candidates attended a fundamental religious denomination, and religious issues had never even surfaced in the election. The candidates were also accused of being uneducated members of the Flat Earth Society, even though one candidate was an accountant, another a business owner who had been previously honored by the school district, and the third a physicist who had written a textbook in that field.

Out of Step

The Colorado Education Association (CEA) found an ally in the People for the American Way (PAW) and donated office space and phones to PAW so they could spread the Religious Right rumors and attempt to sway the election in favor of NEA-approved candidates. Fortunately, this information was leaked to a local paper, the *Rocky Mountain News*, which found the CEA's complicity in such a smear campaign distasteful. In a searing editorial, the *News* stated that such action "makes it clear that the very people who are supposed to be teaching children 'tolerance' are fully aware of the uses of bigotry, and are quite willing to exploit religious intolerance to achieve their goals."[15]

But, the NEA and educational community had been out of step with the general public for a long time. Littleton parents, sick of being ignored, voted in the back-to-basic candidates with an almost two-to-one ratio. However, many teachers do not believe that it is the parent's right to make educational choices for their children. Nor do they remember that it is the parents who employ them. When the three new board members walked up to take their seats at the first meeting of the new board, angry, arrogant teachers stood up, gave the thumbs down sign, and loudly "boo-d" them to the platform.

Unfortunately, electing a new school board cannot reverse almost a century of humanistic influence on schools, teachers, and curriculum. But, it can help, and, in Littleton, the new board succeeded in throwing out the OBE graduation guidelines. Littleton was a national test case for OBE and has provided impetus for the NEA's push for a national school board—in direct violation of the Constitution—which would effectively eliminate any local school control.

Educating the Politically Correct

Not only have the public schools increasingly usurped parental roles, they have also become indoctrination centers for political correctness. Beginning in the earliest grades, children are actively recruited for various causes. Scientifically inaccurate information is fed to students regarding world population growth, global warming, and natural resources until they feel guilty for being human. One text, titled *Save the Earth: An Action Handbook for Kids*, decried the alleged problem of overpopulation, bemoaning that fact that "thousands more are being born every hour" and that the planet cannot support this growth.

> We are using up the earth's resources, like clean air and fresh water, before we have learned to distribute them fairly among all people. We are damaging the earth's environment before we have learned how to restore it. We are changing the earth in ways that may never be undone.[16]

Of course, nothing is said about the fact that people are also dying every hour, making room for new life. Nor does it explain how people should distribute fresh air. Is there now a shortage of oxygen? And, if so, what can a child do about it? The text quickly assures the young recruits that there is one way to save the planet. The answer lies in "the United Nations and in individual countries, in political parties, in large organizations and in small community groups" where people are "marching, protesting, working and finding others to work with them. They are learning how to save the earth. You can join them."[17]

Such texts typically are aimed at playing on the fears of young children. Children are encouraged to sign "save-the-earth" pledges, to support abortion as a cure to overpopulation, to chastise parents for unwise use of resources, and to become militant activists for the environmental movement. Of course, children should be taught to be thrifty and resourceful, but this kind of exploitation is despicable. Children should not be made to feel that their existence is a threat to the survival of earth. No child should be made to feel guilty for being alive.

America the Barbaric

For several decades, schools have sought to undermine national pride. Adventurous explorers are painted as greedy, mass murderers. Children do not know the Pledge of Allegiance or the words to the National Anthem. References to Christianity and its role in civilization has been systematically deleted.

The Pilgrims, who lived in peace and harmony with the native Americans for decades, are portrayed as intolerant bigots. *Amanda's Pilgrims*, an early reader found in a local public school, is a prime example of how these God-fearing settlers are treated. Amanda's younger brother is suffering from nightmares. Convinced that monsters live under his bed, he begs Amanda to switch rooms with him so he can sleep in peace. At first, Amanda refuses, until she has a nightmare that there are Pilgrims under her bed. In her dream, these horrible people force her to work hard, chide her for stopping to watch a butterfly, and punish her for laughing. Shuttering, Amanda wakes up and exchanges rooms with her brother, convinced that the monsters under his bed could not possibly be as evil as the Pilgrims hiding in her room.

America is consistently portrayed as the spoiler of the planet, an international bully, the cause of all famine, war, and pestilence throughout the globe. Little is taught about the massive amounts of foreign aid America has donated or the nations whose liberty has been preserved because American citizens were willing to die for an ideal that all men should be free.

In an ongoing battle to trash American patriotism and promote total disarmament, the horrors of war and nuclear holocaust have become prominent themes in picture books designed for children ages four to seven. One of the mildest books of this kind, found in the children's sections of local elementary school and public libraries, is *Let the Celebrations Begin!*, a story about children in a Nazi concentration camp. The characters, emaciated, starving children with shaved heads, parade cheerfully throughout the story, waiting for the liberating army to come. The book, described on the jacket as "a moving testament to all that is good in mankind," tells the story of women in the camp using scraps of their clothing to make dolls for a celebration party after the war. While it makes a touching story, the Holocaust is not appropriate subject matter for preschoolers. A review in *Time* magazine observed:

> Considering that Auschwitz is the distillation of all that is evil in mankind, the result is a volume of grotesque moral confusion. The very intent of the book—to bring the Holocaust to seven-year-olds without being depressing—is absurd, and so *Celebrations* becomes the reductio ad absurdum of this genre of young people's realism: at once confused, dishonest, disturbing and false.[18]

In *Celebrations*, the Nazis are never identified as the oppressors, nor are the liberators identified as Americans and other allies. But, other books are not so shy. Three books in particular, written in Japan, graphically describe the horrors of war and openly identify America as the great oppressor, destroyer of homes, and murderer of infants.

Faithful Elephants: A True Story of Animals And War describes the destruction of the animals in Tokyo's Ueno Zoo, including the slow starvation death of its three trained elephants. The Japanese Army, concerned that animals might be released on the public as a result of the bombing, had ordered the animal's destruction. The book, designed to move any child to tears, never explains why the "enemy planes" are bombing the city or that the Japanese had begun the war by bombing Pearl Harbor, killing people, not just animals.

Even more graphic are *My Hiroshima* and *Hiroshima No Pika*, which describe the dropping of the atom bomb, complete with illustrations of nude bodies floating through the air, burning and dripping flesh, and dying babies. The perpetrator of such evil is readily identified. "Moments before the Flash, United States Air Force bomber *Enola Gay* had flown over the city and released a top-secret explosive. The explosive was an atomic bomb, which had been given the name 'Little Boy' by the B-29's crew."[19]

No young child should be exposed to the horrors of war; but these books not only expose war, they are incredibly dishonest about it. Children are not told of the atrocities inflicted upon innocent Chinese villagers by the invading hordes of Japanese or how America responded to the invasion with a blockade of Japanese ports in a peaceful attempt to stop the invasion and save thousands of lives. There are no picture books depicting families in Pearl Harbor blown to bits on their way to Sunday school. Nor can you find any mention of the incredible brutalities of the Bataan March. Charles Krauthammer, in his *Time* essay, summed up this form of "children's" literature quite accurately. "These books go beyond the robbing of innocence. They are a perversion of innocence. They don't just forcibly bring the young face to face with evil. They lie about it."[20]

8

Sex in the Classroom

Perhaps the most significant value shift the schools have effected has been the trashing of sexual morality. Even though married couples have enjoyed satisfying sex lives for centuries, educators somehow convinced the public that parents cannot teach their children the facts of life. While the public was told that involving schools in sex education would reduce teen pregnancies, the real motivation behind this incredible marketing job was known in select circles from the beginning. In a 1953 speech before Planned Parenthood workers, Dr. Lena Levine championed using sex education to create what would later be called the Sexual Revolution.

> Our alternative solution is to be ready as educators and parents to help young people obtain sex satisfaction before marriage. By sanctioning sex before marriage, we will prevent fear and guilt. We must also relieve those who have them of their fear and guilt feelings, and we must be ready to provide young boys and girls with the best contraception measures available so they will have

the necessary means to achieve sexual satisfaction without having to risk possible pregnancy. We owe this to them.[1]

Such a blatant admission of Planned Parenthood's
goals was not repeated at PTA or school board
meetings as the controversial topic of sex education
was debated. Most parents remember taking hygiene
classes which consisted of benign films shown to
segregated classes which described the basic biological changes brought about by puberty. But, the
proponents of this sexual revolution were committed to the "task of disseminating these doctrines to
a high-school youth still largely under the sway of
parental influences they considered all too retro-
grade and all too chaste."[2]

Even the most dire predictions of those who
opposed sex education did not foretell the violation
of innocence now being perpetrated against our
youngest children by educators. And, the current
AIDS scare has given educators the needed excuse
to introduce sexual training to the very young.

In 1964, the Sex Information and Education
Council of the United States (SIECUS) was formed
to accomplish this task. Although the name sounds
official, the organization has never carried any governmental sanction. Today SIECUS has become the
nation's largest clearinghouse for information—better known as propaganda—regarding sex in all forms.
SIECUS consistently lobbies for mandated "comprehensive" sex education beginning in kindergarten, and they have produced the most offensive,
grotesque, and desensitizing sex-ed programs available anywhere.

Peggy Brick, president of SIECUS (and, inci-
dentally, an education director for Planned Parenthood), helped compose SIECUS's extensive guide-

lines for comprehensive sexuality education for kindergarten to Grade 12. For children five- to eight-years of age, curriculum should include:

> A family consists of two or more people who care for each other in many ways.
>
> Some couples who love each other live together in the same home without getting married.
>
> People who are married can get divorced when they decide they do not want to live with each other anymore.
>
> Some men and women are homosexual, which means they will be attracted to and fall in love with someone of the same gender.
>
> Touching and rubbing one's own genitals is called masturbation.
>
> Masturbation should be done in private.
>
> All children should be wanted.
>
> Abortion is an option when a baby is not wanted.
>
> Everyone, including children, has rights.[3]

In addition, SIECUS advises, kindergarten students should be told that "it feels good to touch parts of the body . . . and that adults kiss, hug, touch, and engage in other sexual behavior with one another to show caring and to share sexual pleasure."[4]

The *Learning About Family Life* curriculum, written by Barbara Sprung and published by Rutgers University Press, meets these deplorable criteria. In this program, now being used in some public schools, five-year-olds are told exactly what sexual intercourse entails: "The man puts his —— in the woman's ——

and that feels really good for both of them."[5] The philosophical justification put out by SIECUS for such trash is that "the sooner and more completely kids are divested of their innocence in sexual matters, the less vulnerable they will be to repression, victimization, and disease."

Such lies are irresponsible. Raping a child of his or her innocence in this manner should be classified as child abuse. Studies regarding the introduction of "anatomically correct" dolls and child molestation prevention courses confirm that premature information stimulates sexual curiosity and experimentation in children before they are emotionally ready for that aspect of life.

Also, this indoctrination sets kids up for molestation. When molesters attempt to get children to cooperate, they insist the activity will "feel good" and that it is perfectly normal. When a highly regarded teacher gives the same message, it tears down children's natural reluctance and sets them up to become victims.

Open Recruitment

Recommended reading for this age groups also reveals a determined effort to force acceptance of "alternate lifestyles." Included is *Heather Has Two Mommies*, a story of two lesbians and Heather, a little girl conceived through artificial insemination. Heather is very happy but puzzled to discover that other families have a father—that is, until she meets a lucky boy who has two dads. *Gloria Goes to Gay Pride Day* is a book which celebrates "diverse" lifestyles, but somehow omits the debauchery which occurs in public during this annual event.

Lest men should feel neglected, *Daddy's Roommate* rounds out the suggested reading, telling the story of a little boy who spends a weekend visiting his divorced father and the father's male lover. "Daddy and his roommate live together, work together, sleep together, shave together. Daddy and his roommate are very happy together, and I'm happy too," the book proclaims. The jaded mother blissfully explains to her son that "daddy's" lifestyle is perfectly acceptable since there are "different kinds of love." This implausible propaganda piece completely ignores the fact that children are *not* happy when their parents divorce, and women are not too thrilled to be dumped by their husbands for another man.

While proponents of sex education claim that they are not attempting to recruit children to the homosexual lifestyle, the content of some curriculum reveals differently. A California elementary curriculum requires that children "develop an understanding of homosexuality." The *elementary* children are required to watch films which promote the gay lifestyle, engage in homosexual role playing, and be tested on what they learn.

Promoting Promiscuity

Faye Wattleton, president of Planned Parenthood Federation of America, contends that sex education should not focus on morality, but should teach responsible behavior without denigrating sexuality. While she ostensibly objects to "imposing the moral standards of one segment of society on all teenagers," that is *exactly* what these programs accomplish.[6] The instruction designed by SIECUS and others, and approved by Planned Parenthood, has a definite moral theme. These programs openly condone sexual promiscuity and ridicule those who teach chastity. This becomes more apparent in curriculum used for older children.

Between the ages of nine and twelve, SIECUS insists children be taught

> "gay men and lesbians can form families by adopting children or having their own children," and "a legal abortion is very safe." Twelve to 15-year-olds should be taught "sexual orientation cannot be changed by therapy," while 15- to 18- year olds should be given the telephone numbers of local gay and lesbian "help-lines" and should hear that "erotic images in art reflect society's views about sexuality and help people understand sexuality. . . . There is no evidence erotic images in the arts cause inappropriate sexual behavior."[7]

In *Teaching Safer Sex,* Peggy Brick outlines thirty sexual acts evaluated according to HIV risk, including several homosexual activities. These are to be explained in detail to students. Just in case the class should lose interest, or be reluctant to shed their inhibitions, Brick adds a lighter touch. High school teachers are encouraged to throw a "Safer Sex Rock and Roll Dance Party and Trivia," which would require students "to wear a name tag depicting a step in condom use, and to name two rock songs in which condoms are mentioned." Another activity, a Workshop for High Risk Youth, "begins with students shouting pornographic names for sexual organs." (Brick's suggestions are not fit to reprint.)[8]

The Condom Crusade

The AIDS epidemic has given SIECUS and others the weapon they need to pressure parents into sacrificing their children's innocence in an effort to save their lives. Even if a parent does wish to recommend abstinence to their teens, they are still strongly encouraged to teach so-called safe sex techniques. *AIDS-Proofing Your Kids*, by Dr. Loren E. Acker, et. al., a book directed toward concerned parents, devotes one chapter to the topic of abstinence. Though they do give some helpful suggestions, the authors insist that the only way to guarantee safe passage through the teen years is to teach "safe-sex." The rest of the book is devoted to this task, complete with condom games during which the whole family practices proper condom application with firm cucumbers and limp carrots. They suggest that the family member who completes this task fastest win a prize.

Other creative suggestions include giving your child a condom allowance, spreading "sexy" magazines around the house with suggestions on self- and mutual-masturbation, purchasing sex toys for your teens, and ad nauseum. Children should be taught alternatives to actual intercourse, the good doctors agree, and they are quick to supply some suggestions in a section of the book titled "Safe by Sexy: Some Examples."

- Dry kissing
- Body-to-body rubbing
- Telephone sex
- Erotic films, videos, books, magazines
- Body licking and kissing
- Fantasy
- Erotic talk
- Massage/touch/caresses
- Erotic bathing or showering
- Unshared sex toys[9]

Some parents might feel a bit uncomfortable teaching such activities to their children, the authors admit. But fortunately, there is an answer—school-based sex education programs. Parents are urged to support these programs, to insist that their children attend, and to check with the teacher to make certain their teen-ager bares his soul—and modesty—before his peers. A conscientious parent should actively solicit community support for these school programs and should aggressively resist the uninformed, retroactive people in the community who insist that schools stick to academics. "Getting involved with the school in this manner may let you off the hook from discussing sex with your kids. But you'll need an ongoing commitment and involvement with their teachers, because they'll be the ones engaging in the potentially embarrassing discussions."[10]

Sex Ed in Action

When parents abdicate this important responsibility to the schools, however, they are allowing outsiders to set the moral tone for their child's life. The movement to bring "comprehensive sexuality education" is supported by the American Medical Association, the Children's Defense Fund, and Planned Parenthood, all organizations which benefit financially from sexual promiscuity. An examination of New Jersey's *Family Life* program reveals what "comprehensive" education entails.

The New Jersey program, which has been in place for over ten years, begins in kindergarten and gives year-round instruction in anatomy, puberty, reproduction, masturbation, abortion, homosexuality, birth control, sexual assault, and incest. According to the coordinator of the program, Claire Scholz, at first "some of our kindergarten teachers were shy—they didn't like talking about scrotums and vulvas. . . . But now they tell me it's no different from talking about an elbow."[11]

Just how far these condom crusaders will go was demonstrated at a sexuality conference for students held in Guelph, Ontario, in 1990.

> Randy Ruttan, sexual health coordinator for Toronto's board of education, demonstrated a game called the "Condom Line-Up." Students, he explained, should be given pieces of cardboard describing one of several stages of lovemaking with a condom, such as "sexual arousal," "foreplay," "erection," "roll-on condom," "leave room at tip," "intercourse," and so on. Boys and girls are then told to arrange themselves in a line in the correct sequence of behaviours.[12]

Such activities are not isolated incidents, unfortunately. In a school-sponsored "sexuality fair," boys were instructed "to place condoms on their fingers and insert them in plastic models of a vagina." In another session, instructors walked around a room of junior high students, dabbing spermicidal gel on their lips.[13] One fifth-grader in a Colorado school came home very upset after her teacher taught an impromptu condom session. She had passed out condoms to all the girls in the class, instructed the boys to hold up their fingers to resemble their anatomy, and then ordered the girls to pick out a boy to practice on. Parents were not warned about this "instruction" in advance and were unable to rescue their ten-year-old children from this humiliation.

The Department of Education in Virginia adopted a curriculum called *Finding My Way*, which included quizzes on: How to have oral sex, incomplete orgasm, fetishism, what is bestiality, the "moral rightness of homosexuality" between a young boy and an older man, sadism, incest, and rape. Planned

Parenthood, always the leader in this issue, also recommends use of *Boys and Sex* and *Girls and Sex*, two books by Dr. Pomeroy. The lie that sex education is not designed to influence morals is exposed in these texts. Dr. Pomeroy only advocates premarital intercourse by claiming it has "definite value as a training ground for marriage or some other committed relationship."[14]

Dr. Pomeroy goes on to introduce other meaningful forms of sexual expression such as homosexuality and bestiality. "What would happen if a boy had intercourse with an animal? Many farm animals may become a sex object," he muses. In fact, he explains, he has known many boys who had meaningful sexual relationships with various animals. But, if a boy should wish to try this, he would be advised not to tell anyone.[15]

Sex Ed Doesn't Work

The public allowed itself to be railroaded into sexual education on the premise of what Thomas Sowell calls a "Dangerous Myth." He wrote in the *Washington Times*:

> The myth is that "sex education" is a process of giving scientific information to young people as a way of stemming a rising tide of teen-age pregnancy. But the cold fact is that teen-age pregnancy was headed sharply downward before "sex education" programs became entrenched in our schools—and has gone back up afterward, especially where such programs have been most pervasive.[16]

Directors of comprehensive sexuality education programs are reluctant to share any statistical data regarding the effectiveness of these programs, and it's no wonder. The programs have failed miserably in reducing unwanted pregnancies. The fact is, the age of first sexual encounters has dropped and the number of teen abortions and teen births have skyrocketed as sex education has expended. During sex education's first decade, the U.S. government poured over $2 billion into these programs. The payback was a 48.3 percent increase in pregnancies, a 133 percent increase in teen abortions, and an epidemic of sexually transmitted disease, many of them life-threatening.[17]

Abstinence programs, on the contrary, are eager to share their data. *Reducing the Risk*, a program used in some California schools, showed a 24 percent reduction in the odds that participating students would become sexually active in that school year. Studies of a pilot program used in some of Atlanta's public schools, *Postponing Sexual Involvement*, showed that students who enrolled in the class are as much as fifteen times less likely to become sexually active in the following year.

Walking Wounded

The damage caused by this revolt against values is not only physical, but is emotional as well. Teenage romances are notoriously short-lived, and, when sexual activity has been a part of the relationship, it often leaves the young people feeling used and degraded when the relationship ends. During the last twenty years, the number of teen suicides has tripled and the number of young people being admitted into hospitals for depression has doubled. Melvin Anchell, a California psychoanalyst, blames sex education. " 'Typical sex education courses are perfect recipes for producing personality problems and even perversions later in life,' he contends. 'They continuously downgrade the affectionate, monogamous nature of human sexuality.' "[18]

Psychiatrist and writer Thomas Szasz concurs. "Traditionally, sex has been a very private, secretive activity. . . . Herein perhaps lies its powerful force for uniting people in a strong bond. As we make sex less secretive, we may rob it of its power to hold men and women together."[19]

Surveys conducted by Josh McDowell's "Why Wait?" campaign indicate that kids turn to sex in a search for intimacy. And, sex in a committed, monogamous marital relationship does facilitate a special closeness. But, sex-ed programs have effectively reduced this intimate act to casual entertainment. What these classes haven't been able to do is to change man's need for intimacy. The result is a lot of shattered lives.

If SIECUS and Planned Parenthood were really concerned about AIDS, STDs, teen pregnancy, and emotionally healthy young people, it would be logical for them to acknowledge the superiority of abstinence programs over the trash they currently endorse. But, these organizations, which have made billions of dollars selling sex to kids, see anything that resembles traditional morality as a threat to their agendas. So, they lash out at these highly effective programs, branding them as "fear-based curricula" propagated by the "religious right."

When parents in the Stettler School District expressed a desire to throw out the explicit sexual texts for a value-based teen-education program, this so upset the public health "sex experts" that one woman was prompted to write the district's trustees, "warning them about the 'fear-based' abstinence curricula that were making inroads into the province." These dangerous programs were easily iden tifiable, she explained. They "separate boys and girls to discuss sex; depict 'non-traditional families' as 'troubled'; they describe homosexuality as an 'unhealthy choice'; they 'emphasize contraceptive failure rates'; and they don't provide enough 'opportunities for students to explore their own values about premarital sex.' "[20] In other words, these deplorable programs tell the truth.

SIECUS has become so fearful of public reaction to the brazenness of its programs, that it has developed a community advocacy project to deal with backlash from " 'far right' religious zealots." The objectives of this project are "documenting community sex-ed battles around the nation, offering technical assistance, analyzing fear based curricula . . . [and] countering far right challenges."[21]

Value Modification

Sex-ed proponents become angry when the public asks for quantitative measurements to evaluate their effectiveness. In light of their failure rate, this is understandable. " 'Asking if sex education works is almost a meaningless question,' says Martha R. Roper, a health educator from Manchester, Missouri."[22] Her sentiments are shared by other sexuality educators who feel it is unfair to judge the effectiveness of their programs. Robert Selverstone, Ph.D., a sex education teacher in a Westport, Connecticut, high school, admits that their program was never even intended to reduce teen pregnancy. " 'We didn't develop our course with the purpose of reducing teen pregnancy. . . . While it's a worthy goal, that is only one of many components of our program. We are trying to promote healthy sexuality in young people by giving them the skills they need to help them make responsible sexual decisions."[23]

9

Media vs. Morality

Any attempt to critique the media (in less than a favorable light) is invariably met with cries of "Censorship!" But, the cries are disingenuous when coming from an industry which applies censorship to every manuscript, screenplay, or music score it receives. For example, Harper San Francisco, a division of HarperCollins, only publishes 180 of 10,000 submissions they receive each year. Media is business, pure and simple, and what they produce is a product.

When parents discover that a toy has parts which can become dislodged and injure a child, their first reaction is to contact the manufacturer. While their comments may not be appreciated, they are not accused of censorship. If the manufacturer refuses to comply, the parent may go to the press, contact the Consumer Product Safety Commission, have a petition drive, and even threaten a boycott until the defects are resolved. In spite of the ruckus they raise, they are still not accused of censorship. There is a general consensus that manufacturers should be held liable for the quality of their products.

But, when consumers complain to the entertainment industry about the quality of its product, the tables are turned. People who approach the networks with concerns are ridiculed. If consumers band together and threaten to boycott the network's product, they are branded as book-burning, religious zealots who wish to trash the First Amendment and force their views on the world. Unlike other industries, Hollywood and the media apparently feel no responsibility for what they produce.

A typical example of this was Time-Warner's release of a song titled "Cop Killer" in which rap star Ice-T called on fans to "bust some shots off" and "dust some cops off." To begin with, it is illegal to incite anyone to commit murder. Understandably, law-enforcement organizations were incensed at such an irresponsible action that could endanger the lives of police officers. But Time-Warner self-righteously claimed promoting this song was their patriotic duty. That it

> is not a matter of profits, it is a matter of principle. . . . We believe this commitment is crucial to a democratic society, where the full range of opinion and thought—whether we agree with it or not—must be able to find an outlet.[1]

Film critic Michael Medved disagrees. "This line of reasoning is not only unconvincing, it is ultimately insincere. Would Time-Warner have felt the same 'commitment' to providing an 'outlet' for a Ku Klux Klan sympathizer who glorified the shooting of black children?"[2]

Out of Touch

The television and movie industry is sadly out of touch with the values of general America, a fact that is evidenced by the continual drop in customers and profit. Polls conducted by the Associated Press, Gallup Poll, and *Parents Magazine*, among others, all conclude that viewers are not happy with the current state of media entertainment. As many as 82 percent of those polled believed movies were too violent, that they contained too much profanity and nudity, and that the quality of TV programming was getting worse. A *Time*/CNN survey showed that 67 percent of the public believed violent movies were " '*mainly* to blame' for the national epidemic of teenage violence."[3] Those polled also complained about the media's propensity to make fun of religion and marriage.

Comedy clubs, who do not have financial backing of a large studio or network, have also noticed this trend—and are adjusting in order to stay in business. John Cooney, owner of a club called Wit's End, explains,

> I'm a business man and I give the public what they want, not what I think they should get.... My audience [consists of] parents. They have kids and they don't want to hear crass and crude stuff coming off the stage. Clean is the way to go these days. If someone can't be clean and funny, then they're not funny.[4]

Tim Wardwell, owner of the Comedy Club in Aurora, Colorado, agrees: "We book clean, clever comedy. We don't allow gross jokes. We serve a lot of people from the suburbs and they tell me how much they appreciate coming to a club where they're not embarrassed or insulted."[5]

Doing Their Own Thing

Hollywood, however, is obviously not as interested in business as it is in making a point. Studios continuously invest in movies that insult and offend the general public. Some of these, such as *Closetland*, co-produced by none other than Ron Howard (Opie Taylor from "Mayberry, RFD"), was written to make a social statement, not for big returns at the box office. Acclaimed as a challenging work of art, this piece offended even the most hardened entertainment junkie. The entire play is comprised of a vicious male interrogator torturing his female victim. "He forces her to drink his urine, rips her toenails out with pliers, handcuffs her to a bed, spits a half-chewed clove of garlic into her mouth, administers electric shocks to her genitals, and penetrates her anus with a red-hot metal poker as she howls in agony."[6] How can this be justified as artistic expression?

Prime Time

Most of the movie-going public does not waste their time with such avant garde trash as *Closetland*, but the movies billed as family fare and shown on prime time television openly attack the ideals of marriage, fidelity, and God. At a time when sex can kill, actors hop in and out of bed with abandon. And, of course, there are no consequences. And, it's just not the adults who are sleeping around, it's the kids.

But, nowhere is the media bias so strongly exhibited as in the area of religion: networks spend large sums of money consulting with witches (such as Miriam Starhawk), native American shamans, and GLAAD, the Gay and Lesbian Alliance Against Discrimination, so as not to offend or misrepresent the beliefs of their adherents.

As far as Christianity is concerned, however, they spare no expense to offend and alienate. Christians are portrayed as maniacal murderers (*Guilty as Charged*), alcoholic perverts (*At Play in the Fields of the Lord*), and fearfully portray what life would be like if Christians were in charge, complete with public hangings and private whorehouses for the preachers (*The Handmaid's Tale*). Not since the 1930s, when Hitler's propaganda machine took on the Jews, has any religious faith been so viciously attacked and grossly misrepresented by the media.

Aimed at Kids

Obviously aware that they are losing their adult audiences, networks and studios are aiming at children, raising an audience that can be properly trained to accept anything Hollywood wishes to dish out. Defenders of the industry argue that adults decide what they want to watch, therefore the networks are blameless. But, the argument does not take into account the growing number of adolescents who come home from school hours before their parents return from work. Children are the biggest consumers of television, and the media knows it. Preschoolers spend an average of twenty hours of television-viewing a week, grade-school students typically watch twenty-two hours.[7] Another study estimated that by graduation, the average high school student has spent twenty-two thousand hours watching TV, twice as long as he has spent in school in twelve years.[8]

Young children can see movies on television they were not old enough to see in theaters, and the TV promos that advertise them are specifically designed for kids. Every October, for example, toddlers can see the blood-curdling previews of *Nightmare on Elm Street, Friday the Thirteenth, Pet Cemetery*, etc., while watching Disney cartoons. Characters from violent, PG-13 movies adorn lunchboxes and backpacks designed for seven-year-olds. Children, who make up the largest TV viewing audience, are continually bombarded with murder, rape, and brutality. By the time they reach eighteen, they have been exposed to forty thousand murders on television. " 'We teach our children to kill [through the media],' says Deborah Prothrow-Stith, a Harvard University psychologist."[9]

Young children imitate what they see, and they are not always capable of discerning between reality and imagination. If a character behaves in a certain way on television without adverse consequences, then they feel safe to act out in the same way. A prime example of this is MTV's "Beavis and Butt-head," which has been blamed in part for the death of a two-year-old girl. Beavis, one of the grotesque characters of this animated show, has a fixation with setting fires. A five-year-old boy, who for some incomprehensible reason was allowed to watch this trash, decided to imitate Beavis. The tragic consequence was a fire in which his two-year-old sister died. MTV's profane metalloid pals also engage in such delightful pastimes as torturing animals. How many children are imitating that?

While "Beavis and Butt-head" are ostensibly intended for adult audiences, Saturday morning cartoons are definitely intended for the young. It seems ironic, then, that these programs are some of the most violent programs available, featuring more than thirty violent acts per hour—five times the level of prime-time television.[10] Though Christian themes are definitely taboo, children are fed a diet of "Skelator" demons, Gargoyles, and other elements of the occult.

Bad Rap

Michael Billings, Bobby Titsworth, and Stephen and Robert Wartson, ages sixteen to twenty, all pled guilty to the kidnapping and gang rape of two girls from Muskogee High School. The girls, ninth and tenth graders, were taken to a house where the boys took turns raping them and beating them with a belt, all to the tune of "Gangster of Love," a rap song by the Ghetto Boys. District Attorney Drew Edmondson believed the words of the song fueled the sexual assault, and "demonstrated an attitude toward women as basically less than human."[11]

Music is equally as influential on young people as television, with the average teen spending 10,500 hours listening to rock music between the seventh and twelfth grades.[12] Between the two, the media has the attention of our children for much longer periods of time than the parents.

Many parents have bought into the nonsense that music is somehow sacrosanct, that each generation has had their own form of expression, and so it would be unthinkable to place limits in this area. After all, the kids say they just like the music and don't really listen to the words.

But, parents should ask their children to take off the earphones and listen to the lyrics together. The revelation could be startling.

Two current styles of music that are exceptionally violent and destructive are heavy metal and rap.

The words of the most popular songs are too vile to reprint, but the message is appalling. They denigrate women; debase sex; and promote perversions, rape, promiscuity, sadism, and murder. The original cover for the Guns N' Roses album, *Appetite for Destruction*, featured a rape scene. This delightful artwork was reprinted on T-shirts for ardent fans to display.

One of the most profane albums to be released is 2 Live Crew's *Nasty As They Wanna Be*. Richard DeMoss, Jr., youth culture specialist for Focus on the Family, transcribed this double record set and found

- 87 descriptions of oral sex
- 117 explicit references to male and female genitalia
- 226 uses of the "F"-word
- 163 uses of b—— when referring to women
- 81 uses of the vulgarity sh——
- 42 uses of the word a——[13]

The album also included several references to incest, group sex, and over a dozen illustrations of violent sexual acts.

When criticism is aimed at vulgar rap, many performers instantly level the charge of racism. But, leaders within the black community don't buy that argument and don't want race to be used as a defense for pornography. When 2 Live Crew tried to deflect criticism this way, the National Association for the Advancement of Colored People (NAACP) was quick to respond:

> "We are particularly offended by their efforts to wrap the mantle of the black cultural experience around their performances by saying this is the way it is in the black

community, and that they are authentic pur-
veyors of our heritage," declared Dr. Benjamin Hooks. "Our cultural experience does
not include debasing our women, the glori-
fication of violence, the promotion of devi-
ant sexual behavior, or the tearing into shreds
of our cherished mores and standards of
behavior."[14]

Does Message Count?

Media executives continually assert that their
products merely represent society. And, anyway, they
shrug, no one has ever proven that viewing rape,
murder, decapitation, and other forms of violence
has ever had a negative effect on anyone. But, this
is ludicrous.

To begin with, movies do not represent real
life. Rothmann, Lichter, and Lichter reviewed more
than six hundred prime-time programs to see if
media claims were justified. The conclusion: "Violent crime is far more pervasive on television than
in real life, and the disparity widens as the danger
increases. . . . Since 1955 television characters have
been murdered at a rate one thousand times higher
than real-world victims."[15] Michael Medved observes,
"Hollywood, in other words, does more than recre-
ate real-world brutality; it glorifies violence as an
enjoyable adventure and a manly ideal."[16]

Almost one thousand studies have been conducted to determine if viewing violence affects behavior, and the consensus is in: a resounding yes!
According to Carol Lieberman of the National
Coalition on Television Violence, these studies "show
[a] 95 percent causal link between violent entertainment and subsequent harmful behavior. . . . The
[only] studies that don't show this are funded mostly

by TV networks."[17] A study conducted by a California medical association indicated that as many as 22 percent of juvenile crimes had been suggested by television programs.[18]

Suggestions of this link can be found in some of the more brutal juvenile crimes. In Boston, a gang forced a woman to douse herself with gasoline and then set her on fire after watching the exact crime on television two days earlier. In Utah, three people died after being forced to drink drain cleaner. The murderers had no apparent motive for the crime, but, on the day of the murder, they had watched *Magnum Force* three times. In one scene a prostitute was murdered by being forced to drink drain cleaner.[19] After watching the main character in *The Executioner's Song* murder his grandparents, Jeffrey Alan Cox killed his own grandparents in the same manner. In 1984, after *The Deerhunter* was released, twenty-eight people killed themselves playing Russian roulette after watching the movie.[20]

Does that mean everyone will imitate every crime they see? Of course not, but it does show the influence the media has to instigate action, and this is particularly true with young children who do not have an established value set and people who are already at risk for violent behavior.

Psychologists overwhelmingly agree with the obvious, that people are affected by the images and ideas they put into their minds. A steady diet of violence and promiscuity *does* affect personal values, and, as movies and television compete with one another for shock value, the damage is even worse. According to University of Illinois psychologist Leonard Eron, "The more realistic the violence is, the more effect it has, because the youngster thinks that everybody acts this way and that it is an appro-

priate way to go about solving problems. Children
model their behavior after these characters, particularly if they're seen in a positive light."[21]

The Role of Music

Nathan McCall, a black *Washington Post* reporter
who spent three years in prison for armed robbery,
reiterates the affect media had on his choices as a
young man. And, though he applauds efforts to
control violence on television and in the movies, he
is even more concerned about the negative impact
of gangsta rap on young blacks, pointing to the
lyrics of a song by Dr. Dre that calls for black men
to kill one another. McCall argues:

> It may seem crazy to tie music to behavior.
> But the history of African-Americans shows
> that, from the days of slavery to the present,
> music has always been an agent of change.
> And rap is more than rhyming words. It's
> the central part of a powerful cultural move-
> ment—hip-hop—that influences the way young
> blacks walk, talk, dress and think.[22]

Na'im Akbar, former president of the Association of Black Psychologists, believes the negative
messages in the media correlate with an increase in
youth violence. For example, since the late 1980s
the incidents of black-on-black crime have increased
dramatically, in direct correlation with the sudden
surge in popularity of gangsta rap.[23]
Melvin Williams of the District of Columbia
Commission on Mental Health Services believes rap
is a powerful influence on at-risk youth. "While the
vast majority of kids are able to take negative rap
and put it in perspective, some of our most vulnerable ones are influenced. Those young people who

have faulty parenting or no parenting at all are particularly vulnerable to influences such as rap."[24]

The hypocrisy of media claims that people are not influenced by what they see and hear is glaringly apparent when they begin to sell advertising. If the public is immune to their messages, then how can they in good conscience charge millions of dollars for advertising slots during the Super Bowl? The marketing executives at Coca-Cola, Pepsi, MCI, Proctor and Gamble do not support television out of a spirit of generosity; they do it because it pays. People buy what they see.

Uncle Sam Foots the Bill

For the past few years, it has become fashionable for Congress to hold hearings about violence and pornography in the media. This is particularly ironic, however, considering Congress has repeatedly voted to fund the worst displays of both through the National Endowment for the Arts (NEA).

The national budget is out of control, and the deficit continues to rise, yet any attempt to stop funding the "arts" or to even set standards for how the money will be spent is met with accusations of censorship. It is argued that the government should not be in the business of controlling the arts. Rep. Dana Rohrabacher (R-Calif.) claims,

> Those who truly oppose Government control of the arts should oppose Government funding of the arts. Money for the arts should be left with the people, rather than taxed away, so they can make their own free determination as to what art they will or will not support, rather than giving that power to the state.[25]

Donations of tax dollars to the NEA continue, even though the works they support are profane, pornographic, sacrilegious, and at times even criminal. The NEA argues against censorship, yet it routinely practices censorship by refusing to fund decent work in favor of trash. In 1989, the NEA denied a ten thousand dollar grant to the New York Academy of Art for teaching young painters basic skills. The NEA claimed "teaching students to draw the human figure is revisionist . . . and stifles creativity." A short time later, the endowment used seventy thousand dollars of tax funds to sponsor a gallery show featuring Shawn Eichman's "Alchemy Cabinet," a display which included a jar containing the remains of Eichman's own abortion.[26]

Frederick Hart, the sculptor responsible for the *Three Soldiers* statue at the Vietnam War Memorial was turned down for a grant to complete a series of "Creation Sculptures." The NEA informed him his work did not constitute art. At the same time, however, they awarded twenty thousand dollars of tax funds for a project in a park whose goal was "to create large, sexually explicit props covered with a generous layer of requisitioned Bibles."[27]

Other illustrious projects sponsored by the Endowment for the Arts and paid for with tax funds include grants to performer John Fleck, who urinates on a picture of Christ on stage, and to Annie Sprinkle, who masturbates on stage with several sex toys and invites the audience to join her.

Joel-Peter Witkin has received four NEA fellowship awards since 1980, totaling over fifty thousand dollars. His "works of art" include photographs of severed genitalia, arms, limbs, and dead fetuses. He also boasts pictures titled *Woman Castrating a Man, Arm F—* (which shows a man with his arm inserted past the elbow into the rectum of another man), and numerous antireligious depictions, including a photo of actual crucified monkeys on either side of a naked man in a crucifix position. Though torturing animals in this manner is illegal, Witkin was paid by Congress for doing it.

Another bizarre entry was a photograph called *The Kiss*. To create this unique piece, Witkin paid a pathologist to decapitate an unclaimed body from the county morgue. He then severed the head in half and positioned it so that the corpse appeared to be kissing himself.

Other disturbing projects funded by taxpayers through the NEA include a photo display of Mapplethorpe's which should have resulted in charges of child molestation. This is a crime punishable by imprisonment, yet no one will touch the perpetrators and make any attempt to find and rescue the poor children who were destroyed for this "art." After all, the United States Congress paid the bill.

As long as the highest legislative body in America is willing to pay for "entertainment" that even television executives are reluctant to display, we cannot expect things to change. If art does imitate life, then America is in trouble.

10

The Family under Siege

Our nation's history is steeped in a rich tradition of family. Alexis de Tocqueville, who was accustomed to the moral laxness prevalent in some European circles, marveled at American fidelity. Strong families, he observed, were an outgrowth of spiritual values and the foundation of a stable government.

> There is certainly no country in the world where the tie of marriage is more respected than in America or where conjugal happiness is more highly or worthily appreciated. In Europe almost all the disturbances of society arise from the irregularities of domestic life.[1]

It is from family that children receive a sense of roots, learn self-discipline, and acquire moral values: essential elements in developing healthy self-esteem. Strong homes build strong children and in turn, a strong community.

But, in America, the family has taken a beating.

Epidemic of Divorce

For centuries, divorce was seen in most cultures as a public statement of failure, an avenue of last resort. Marriage vows were taken seriously, and laws often required divorcing couples with children to present compelling cause for dissolving a marriage. Many struggling marriages remained intact "for the sake of the kids." Throughout the fifties, less then ten out of every one thousand marriages in America would end in divorce each year.[2]

This attitude changed drastically with the cultural revolution of the sixties. A "live for the moment" attitude prevailed, and commitment to anything besides self-satisfaction was out of vogue. Monogamy was viewed as a hateful institution, created by chauvinistic men to keep women in bondage and submission. The result was a sharp increase in divorce rates beginning in 1965 and peaking at twenty-three per one thousand in 1974. The current rate is approximately twenty-one divorces per one thousand marriages.[3] Over one million Americans see their parents divorce each year, and ten million children live in single family homes.[4]

The age-old wisdom that children thrive better in an intact, two-parent family was swept aside by feminists and sociologists who no longer chose to view the traditional family as a valuable institution. One popular divorce book insisted, "A two-parent home is not the only emotional structure within which a child can be happy and healthy. . . . The parents who take care of themselves will be best able to take care of their children."[5] The message was unmistakable, a parent's happiness came first, the needs of the children came last.

The importance of men to the family structure and to society in general was downplayed, reflecting an attitude voiced by Gloria Steinem: "A woman without a man is like a fish without a bicycle." Children were resilient, divorce books insisted, and would suffer no permanent damage as a result. In fact, it could be a life-enriching experience, giving the child two happy homes instead of one.[6]

Another taboo lifted during this era was childbearing out of wedlock. The illegitimacy rate has doubled since 1970, and, in some neighborhoods, half of all children are born to single mothers, increasing the number of single-parent homes from four million to eight million.[7]

These societal trends have been glamorized and even promoted by the media. After throwing off the Motion Picture Code, the industry seemed to launch a frontal assault against marriage and fidelity. Extramarital affairs appeared in one out of thirty evening television shows (daytime TV has been raunchy for a long time), but that ratio has now narrowed to at least one out of six. In fact, the average television viewer watches fourteen thousand references to sex each year, and most of these are extramarital.[8]

When marriage does hit the silver screen, it is quite often portrayed as a sick, unfulfilling, abusive, and even murderous institution. Afternoon talk show hosts compete with one another to see who can reveal the deepest, dirtiest secrets, with enlightening topics such as "mothers who stole their daughter's boyfriends," and "the value of infidelity," etc. A steady diet of television could lead viewers to believe that healthy, monogamous marriages no longer existed.

Those doubts are further fueled by the deliberately erroneous claim that half of all marriages end in divorce. This conclusion was drawn from U.S.

Census Bureau reports in 1981: a record 1,213,000 divorces occurred. That same year, there were 2,422,000 marriages. But, the only way those numbers could represent a 50 percent divorce rate would be if every married couple alive in America had applied for a license in 1981. Numerous polls indicate that marriage is still considered an important, lifetime commitment by the majority of married adults. The 50 percent claim is widely publicized, however, in an apparent attempt to convince Americans that traditional families are dead, thereby gaining support for "alternative" families.

Hollywood is not alone in its vilification of the family. Books, such as *The Way We Never Were: American Families and the Nostalgia Trap* by Stephanie Coontz, attempt to portray monogamous marriages of the forties and fifties as nothing more than "booze, bowling, bridge, and boredom."[9] An art show in Boston featuring a display called "Good-bye to Apple Pie" contained several artists' renditions of child abuse, including a mixed media piece titled *Father Knows Best*, which showed several knives sticking out of a small girl's dress. Barbara Whitehead writes of seeing a bumper sticker in Amherst, Massachusetts, which read, "UNSPOKEN TRADITIONAL FAMILY VALUES: ABUSE, ALCOHOLISM, INCEST."[10] This kind of propaganda is not only offensive, it is blatantly untrue. Abuse does occur, and so does incest, but not in the majority of families. Inflated statistics are used by Child Protection Agencies to shore up their power and ensure continued financing. As many as 80 percent or more of all abuse reports are false, and, of the remaining, only a few should result in removal of a child. Incest makes up approximately 3 percent of all abuse reports, and most of the time the perpetrator is not a blood parent.[11]

Kids Ignored

There are times when divorce is necessary, such as in cases of spousal or child abuse. No one should be required to live in a dangerous setting with a person who refuses to change his behavior. A spouse should not be expected to tolerate infidelity. However, most divorces today are not based on these situations, but on what parents view as being in their best interest. All too often, the needs of the kids are ignored.

Children overwhelmingly oppose divorce. A survey conducted by the "Why Wait?" campaign discovered that the number one desire of teens between the ages of eleven and fifteen is to have a happy home with both parents. Seventy-five percent of the young people questioned felt divorces were too easy to obtain, and three-fourths of the children from broken homes were convinced that their parents had not tried hard enough to resolve their differences.[12]

In addition, children are often called upon to meet the emotional needs of their parents, a reversal in roles no young person is equipped to handle. *Dinosaurs Divorce: A Guide for Changing Families* was written as a survival guide for very young children experiencing divorce. The tragedy of the shattered home is illustrated with green dinosaurs' parents who "fight, drink too much, and break up," comforting subject matter for toddlers. The book explains that the child will no longer be able to live with both parents and may have to leave his home and friends because of reduced financial resources. "Living with one parent almost always means there will be less money. Be prepared to give up some things."

The poor kid, who is still suffering from his parent's separation, is introduced to the concept of a stepfamily and warned to be nice to stepparents, regardless of their personal feelings. The message to a hurting child is that they are to be understanding, respectful, and polite to troubled parents, yet no attention is given to the child's incredible loss or pain.[13] Such a message is selfishness taken to the extreme.

When a divorce does occur, children suffer greatly from the broken relationships with both parents. Mothers, who are usually granted custody, must work outside the home to make ends meet, giving them less quality time with the children. In addition, they often resume dating and social lives, reducing even more the precious time together. Noncustodial parents are almost totally removed from any significant input into their children's lives. When visits are restricted to every other weekend, the influence of that parent (usually the father) is severely jeopardized.

The Verdict Is In

After twenty years of being told children are not negatively impacted by divorce, empirical data is now available to prove what society has known for centuries: kids need two parents.

Several studies were begun in the early seventies to monitor the long-term impact of divorce upon kids. Psychologist Nicholas Zill conducted an eleven-year study which documented the detrimental effect divorce had on the relationship between children and noncustodial fathers, even if the father had faithfully honored visitation.[14] Sara McLanahan, a sociologist for Princeton University's Woodrow Wilson School, became disturbed after reading a series which portrayed single mothers as a significant cause of the growing underclass in America. This went against the conventional wisdom of the seventies, so McLanahan decided to conduct a study of her own. The results, which she later published with Irwin Garfinkel in *Single Mothers and Their Children*, gave overwhelming testimony to the financial plight of single moms. Half of all single mothers in the United States live below the poverty level, and, for most, this is not a temporary situation. Many women do not receive support and do not remarry, which in turn makes them even more dependent upon welfare.[15]

For unwed mothers, the welfare trap is particularly difficult to escape. Single mothers stay on welfare longer than any other recipient. Of those who have never been married, almost 40 percent will spend ten years or more on the welfare rolls.[16] Most of these women do not receive any support from the child's father and are likely to stay unmarried. In fact, a condition for receiving benefits is that the mother remain unmarried and basically unemployed.

If support is received from the father, it is generally not enough to completely care for the needs of the family, an obvious consequence since the father's income is now split between the maintenance of two homes. In 1982, when this study was conducted, approximately 60 percent of white single mothers and 80 percent of black single mothers received no income from their children's father. For those who did receive child support and alimony, the average amount received per month by white women was $1,246, while their black counterparts were only given $322.[17] In the mid-1980s stricter standards were set in place that increased

the amount of child support awarded in a divorce
settlement, and additional options for collecting
payments were put in place. Delinquent fathers can
find their income tax refunds rerouted to former
spouses or welfare agencies, and they may also have
their paycheck garnished, provided the ex-wife knows
where they work. Yet, the majority of single mothers still do not receive child support.

Self-perpetuating Cycle

Another disturbing finding was that children
from welfare-dependent, mother-only homes have a
much greater likelihood of perpetuating that situation in their own lives. The statistics are staggering.

> Among white families, daughters of single
> parents are 53 percent more likely to marry
> as teenagers, 111 percent more likely to have
> children as teenagers, 164 percent more likely
> to have a premarital birth, and 92 percent
> more likely to dissolve their own marriages.[18]

Among black and other minority communities,
the numbers are even higher and have had a devastating effect upon those cultures. All of these factors tend to increase dependency to welfare and
reduce the probability of ever becoming financially
dependent. Teens, who make up the largest segment of unmarried parents, are especially vulnerable. Approximately 15 percent of teen-age moms
will become pregnant again within one year, and 30
percent will conceive again in two years.[19] Many
young mothers drop out of high school, and, of
those who graduate, only 5 percent get college
degrees, as compared to 47 percent of the women
who put off childbearing until after their education
is complete.[20] Without sufficient education and train-

ing, these young women are unqualified to compete for higher paying jobs. Many mothers with more than one child receive more from welfare than they can earn on minimum wage. There are no work requirements tied to receiving government aid. In fact, if they do try to work, their benefits may be cut one dollar for every dollar earned. This situation effectively destroys any incentive to become self-sufficient and has created what some have described as a culture of dependency. According to Ann Clark, a welfare caseworker, "The federal government has created a monster. I'm dealing with third-generation recipients. Welfare has become their way of life. It scares them to death to try to get off it."[21]

Devastating Consequences

The breakdown of the nuclear family is a major cause of the increase in juvenile problems. Seventy percent of juvenile offenders come from single-parent homes.[22] The majority of children in gangs come from abusive family situations or from homes which do not have a significant male role model. While a stable single-parent home is better than a dangerous two-parent one, boys still need male role models to develop a sense of who they are as a man. Many turn to gangs for that identity. Children need consistent boundaries, discipline, security, and love from a family. Those who do not get that are more likely to use drugs and alcohol, search for love and intimacy through sexual activity, and develop depression.

Studies of children of divorce have also shown that they exhibit more anger, have less developed social skills, get in trouble at school more, and have lower grades. Other effects noted are lower self-esteem and a greater sense of withdrawal from society.[23]

The Missing Dad

One of the devastating consequences of divorce and illegitimacy is that millions of American children are growing up without fathers. In spite of the rhetoric from radical feminists, psychologists now agree that the presence of a father is extremely important to children. Fathers serve as role models and authority figures. Some children born to unmarried mothers never have any contact with their natural fathers. In cases of divorce, even when a noncustodial father remains in contact with his children, his role and influence are significantly altered. Children do not simply need advice and instruction every other weekend. They learn values and discipline through daily interaction. When noncustodial dads do get to see their kids, they generally want to make the most of it. They go to movies, amusement parks, and various other activities, which make for good memories, but it cannot replace the daily living that develops closeness.

More and more, however, fathers who leave their families do not maintain close contact with their children. The National Survey of Children revealed that in disrupted families, only one child in six had seen his or her father weekly in the last year. As time goes on, fathers often become caught up in their own lives, and the contact with their children declines. Ten years after a divorce, more than two-thirds of the children had not seen their fathers in over a year.[24]

The importance of a close father-child relationship can be seen by what happens to children when that relationship does not exist. As stated earlier, the absence of a father can lead to involvement in crime, gangs, and destructive behavior. But, even those children who do not become delinquents, who stay in school, and by all outward appearances seem to be doing fine are affected. A study was conducted by 1,337 medical doctors, who were alumni of John Hopkins, to determine if there was any common causal factors between stress-related diseases such as hypertension, coronary heart disease, malignant tumors, mental illness, and suicide. Only one common factor was discovered: a lack of close relationships with parents, especially fathers. In another study, thirty-six out of thirty-nine girls suffering from anorexia lacked a close relationship with their fathers.[25]

Girls who grow up without fathers tend to become involved sexually at an earlier age than girls from intact families, regardless of racial or economic barriers. This was confirmed in studies by John Hopkins University, which found that "young, white, teenage girls living in fatherless families . . . were 60 percent more likely to have had intercourse than those living in two-parent homes."[26] In response to the question "Why do teens have sex?" one youth responded:

> The reason I see as the most common for sex before marriage is the overwhelming need to be close to another human being, to make emotional contact, to gain a sense of self-worth, to keep from being lonely and to feel cared for.[27]

Working Moms

Another change families have undergone over the past three decades has been an exodus of mothers from the home. Between 1950 and 1981, the number of working mothers tripled. Dr. Ken Magid, a psychologist with St. Joseph Hospital in Denver, comments, "Never in the history of the world have so many children been raised by strangers."[28] Some women, wishing to pursue a career, have chosen to join the work force voluntarily. But, for many families, two paychecks are a necessity. Part of this is due to increased costs of living and a subsequent loss in buying power. For example, according to the Department of Housing and Human Services, inflation-adjusted income for a married couple decreased from $30,947 in 1973 to $27,000 in 1990.[29] An even greater factor, however, is the increase in taxation. In 1950, workers paid approximately 2 percent of their gross income in federal taxes. The combined total of all taxes—federal, state, and local—was just over 5 percent. With the majority of the income coming home, most mothers could afford to stay home and raise their children if they wished. Now, combined taxation devours over 45 percent of a family's gross income, making life with one paycheck more challenging. Many moms are working to support Uncle Sam.

Discussions of the benefits of stay-at-home moms invariably raise protest from feminists, who quickly point to full-time motherhood as instituted male domination. They create a perception that full-time childrearing is somehow stifling and unfulfilling, a choice no woman in her right mind would make willingly.

But, the feminist ideology is not shared by a large number of mothers, as *Redbook* discovered when it asked readers, "Do children need a stay-at-home mother?" Letters poured in from all over the nation. Women between the ages of twenty and fifty years old responded. Some had no children, others had as many as six, giving the survey a good demographics representation. The editors of *Redbook* were amazed at the results.

Overwhelmingly, respondents favored a woman staying home with her small children. Not surprisingly, 74.5 percent of nonworking mothers agreed that when a mother works outside the home, her children almost always suffer. But 49.5 percent of the working mothers also held that opinion.[30]

Day Care Woes

It has been known for some time that sociopathic personalities are created when children fail to form close bonds to an adult in the first two or three years of life. These children grow up to be angry, manipulative people incapable of bonding emotionally with anyone. Sociopaths feel no guilt or remorse for their actions and go through life leaving a path of emotional destruction in their wake. Some, like Robert Sandifer, become criminals.

Psychologists and criminologists have become alarmed at the increasing numbers of juveniles who commit senseless, brutal violence, yet exhibit absolutely no remorse when caught. Numerous studies have been performed to determine what has changed in our society to cause this. The results point conclusively to changes in family stability. Abuse, neglect, and the lack of strong father figures can create "unattached children," kids who are at risk for becoming sociopaths.

But, unattached kids are becoming a growing phenomenon in intact families as well, and evidence indicates that early day care may be the primary culprit. Numerous studies, such as those conducted by Alison Clarke-Steward, a psychology professor at the University of California at Irvine, and Dr. Ron Haskins of the University of North Carolina, appear to confirm this, documenting the negative effects of day care on young children. These children showed much more avoidance to their parents, aggressive behavior toward each other, and resistance to adult authority.[31]

The younger the child is when he enters day care, the greater the potential harm. This is especially true in regular day-care centers, where children receive little physical affection. Concerned about a rash of false abuse charges, most child care workers are instructed not to hug, hold, or kiss the children in their care. However, those physical displays of affection are essential for bonding. Child development specialist Edward F. Zigler and Yale University warns that "infants put in day-care centers may be harmed by sensory deprivation and trauma caused by separation from their mothers, comparable to 'psychological thalidomide.'"[32]

After twenty years of research in this area, educational psychologist Doctor White is convinced that children should spend most of their waking hours with a full-time parent or other loving relative during their first three years of life.[33]

For many American families, however, this is not an option.

The Destruction of the Black Family

No other culture in our society has been as devastated by family disintegration than the black community. Black Americans have had an incredible heritage of family, and the presence of so many single-parent homes is a relatively new phenomenon. Before the Civil War, single-parent families were a result of slavery, not choice. When given the opportunity, many slaves would risk death attempting to escape rather than to be separated from family members. After the Civil War, family and religion continued to be pillars of the black community. A

1905 survey conducted in New York found only one single black mother with more than one child out of fifteen thousand families. Two-parent families remained the norm until after World War II.[34]

During the early part of the century, unemployment rates among blacks were much lower than among whites—partly due to the lower wages blacks received and partly due to a strong work ethic. But, something has drastically altered the structure of the black community. After forced segregation was removed, middle class blacks moved out of the inner cities, seeking opportunities not available previously. Before this time, the black community had been more balanced, Ted Travis, director of Neighborhood Ministries in Denver explains. A child might come from a poor, fatherless family, but there were also lawyers, doctors, and other members of the middle class living on his block. Though he might not have a male role model at home, there were enough successful black men in the neighborhood to make him believe that progress was possible.

Those who left the community did fairly well, as a survey published by the Joint Center for Political Studies, a Washington-based black political think tank, revealed. Joseph Perkins reported in the *Wall Street Journal* in 1988 that the black middle class had grown by nearly a third since 1980 and the number of black professionals had jumped 63 percent. The number of black managers and corporate officers had also increased 30 percent during that same time period.[35]

In spite of these positive advances, the plight of those left behind in the inner cities is drastically different. In inner-city ghettos, unemployment rates among black youth is 40 percent, and one-fourth of the men between the ages of twenty and twenty-four have essentially "dropped out of the economy," not working, looking for work, or going to school. The increase in illegitimate children has resulted in a 100 percent increase in the number of families dependent upon welfare. The proportion of two-parent black families has decreased from 64 percent in 1970 to only 39 percent in 1990. Only one black student in seven receives scores above the fiftieth percentile on college placement tests.[36] In some neighborhoods, 80 percent of black children are born to single parents.[37]

But, the most tragic statistics are the crime rates. Approximately half of the nation's prison population is black, even though they comprise only one-tenth of the population. Murder has become the leading cause of death for young blacks. Almost 40 percent of all of our nation's murder victims are black men who have been killed by other blacks.[38] In Washington, D.C., more that 40 percent of black males between the ages of eighteen and thirty-five are involved in some capacity with the criminal justice system.[39]

What Went Wrong

The problems of the poor black community are a result of family breakdown, a damaged work ethic, and lost hope, caused in large part by social welfare programs ostensibly created to wipe out poverty forever. Instead, these programs trap people into a form of slavery that may be more effective at wiping out a culture than any other form of slavery in the past.

Between the mid-1940s and mid-1960s, poverty rates had been cut in half. In 1962 President Kennedy declared war on poverty, creating a public welfare system to accomplish this purpose. Lyndon

Johnson continued the tradition with his plans for a "Great Society" in which poverty would be eradicated if enough money was thrown at the problem.

These programs did not eliminate poverty, however. In fact, they did just the opposite, creating an underclass "trapped in a culture that teaches them not to work and not to hope for better than they have."[40] Aid to Families with Dependent Children (AFDC), a noble sounding program, guaranteed a monthly income to women (or teens) who had children, regardless of age. The only guidelines were that the woman could not get married and could not work. Girls who could not afford to move away from home now were offered an avenue. Get pregnant, stay single, don't get a job, and you will get food stamps, housing assistance, and a monthly check. Struggling two-family homes could also get assistance if the husband would move out. Some poor took this option, thinking their marriages would survive the "temporary" absence. Often, it did not, and the family remained on the welfare rolls.

Men Not Needed

The result was a devastating breakdown of morals and family among poor blacks, the cultural foundation which had seen them through incredible adversities in the past. "Millions of men and women whose parents, grandparents, and great-grandparents managed to survive centuries of war, dislocation, slavery, oppression, and poverty have had generations of traditional values and habits destroyed during a few decades."[41]

Jawanza Kunjufu, an expert on black culture, describes the implementation of these programs as the planned destruction of the black man; an examination of welfare at work lends credence to his

assessment. Liberal programs offered great promise
and guaranteed political votes, but they have almost
destroyed a people.

A group of young black girls meeting at Neighborhood Ministries was asked if their father lived at
home with the family. Only one girl out of eight
could raise her hand. The other seven remarked
that their fathers had never lived with them or had
left at an early age. When the speaker asked how
their mothers described their fathers, the answers
were anything but positive. Without exception the
girls had heard their mothers say, "I don't need that
man." When asked how that affected their opinions
of men, the girls seemed negative as well. They all
seemed to want a family, but they were reluctant to
ever live with a man.

The message this carries to a young inner-city
black male growing up in a female-dominated home
is clear. They are not needed. If mom doesn't need
his father, why would any family need him? Most of
his friends are also fatherless, so there is no one to
model to him how to be a provider and nurturer.
He has no identifiable role in his society.

Lost Hope

"Without vision, the people perish," the Bible
warns. People can endure incredible hardship if they
have hope, if they can keep alive a dream for the
future. It was this incredible human capacity for
hope that helped thousands to survive the depriva-
tions of wars and famines. It was hope that kept
people alive in Nazi prison camps.

Hope is a uniquely human characteristic, a special gift. Children are born dreamers. Small children are filled with plans of what they will accomplish in life. As they grow older, however, they look

at the people around them, judging their own ability to succeed by the success of others. They become increasingly aware of the obstacles and of perceived limits. If they do not see a way to overcome those obstacles, hope is lost.

According to Kunjufu, this loss of hope occurs in black inner-city males somewhere between the third and fifth grades. At that age, children become more aware of their surroundings. Everywhere they look is poverty. The people with money are drug dealers. Most kids living in the ghetto have known someone who has been murdered, but they know few people who have succeeded. Life expectancy for a young black man in the ghetto is twenty-five. With no men to model successful lifestyles, these young people assume it is out of their reach. They give up.

The Assault Continues

For three decades, we have been performing an experiment with the American family. The result has been dismal failure. Yet, the pressure to continue this destructive path continues.

In spite of much rhetoric, nothing has been done to alter the structure of the institutional slavery known as welfare. Congress continues to provide financial support for pornography. States across the nation have mandated sex education in their schools, in spite of mounting evidence that these programs cause promiscuity. Curriculum stressing abstinence, the only medically safe option for teens in the age of AIDS, is forbidden as "religious." Books on homosexuality can be found in high school libraries while the Bible is banned.

Children thrive best with a stay-at-home parent, yet the prevalence of single-parent families and oppressive taxation eliminates this possibility for many families. The solution proposed by liberal politicians like Patricia Schroeder (D-Colo.) is not to cut taxes or to change welfare incentives. Instead, they propose letting the government care for our children in state-run child care centers. Even parents who stay at home are being pressured to bring their families under government scrutiny through programs such as Parents as First Teacher, where social workers enter the home, monitor the "stimulation" offered in the home, and inform parents what methods of discipline they may use. Children in grade schools are encouraged to report their parents if they get a spanking and to write essays about topics such as "What my parents fight about."

Wards of the State

In 1974, Congress passed the Federal Child Abuse Prevention and Treatment Act, otherwise known as the Mondale Act. This law was supposed to put an end to child abuse and dysfunctional families. Instead, it created a monstrous system of child protective agencies, which destroys both children and families. Anonymous reporting was encouraged, and anyone with an ax to grind could turn in a false charge of child abuse against anyone—anonymously and with full immunity. Untrained social workers were given power to violate constitutional rights, becoming judge, jury, and executioner. Parents can be permanently stripped of all rights to their children without ever being charged with a crime and without ever having a trial by jury. Parents who are charged with child abuse and found innocent in criminal court are sometimes shocked to discover that the state can still allow someone else to adopt their children. Foster care was removed from the private sector and put under government control. The result: a child is now ten times more likely to be abused or molested in foster care than in the general public. As juvenile crime soars, the government continues to pour money into programs that simply do not work.

At a time when young people desperately need discipline, social services agencies are allowed to dictate what form that discipline may take. There is a concerted effort to make any form of corporal punishment a crime, even though no data exists which would indicate that spanking, when used with discretion, has ever caused any harm. In fact, as spanking has gone out of vogue, the incidence of violence has increased.

Parents who use other methods of discipline are also at risk for abuse charges. Children have been removed from homes because a twelve-year-old was not allowed to wear make-up to school, because a pregnant fourteen-year-old was grounded from seeing her gang-member boyfriend, and because a young teen lost phone privileges after coming home late. Instead of empowering parents, government programs and policies seem bent on destroying the family completely.

Child's Rights vs. Family Autonomy*

Over the last two decades there has been a growing misconception that the rights of parents and children are somehow incompatible. Unfortunately,

---

*A more complete discussion of this topic may be found in *Out of Control: Who's Watching our Child Protection Agencies* by Brenda Scott, published by Huntington House Publishers, 1994.

this philosophy has invaded the White House. As early as 1979, Hillary Clinton (then Rodham) went on record defending children's rights to self-determination.

As this philosophy has gained momentum, the authority of parents to promote values, set guidelines, enforce discipline, limit social contacts, and make educational choices has been continually attacked. Social service agencies have destroyed families over the use of corporal punishment, curfews, dress codes, and homeschooling. In fact, the New York State Council of Family and Child Caring Agencies warns that parents who resist state interference, believe in spanking, or display an "over involvement in religion" are suspect.

Traditionally, family rights have been protected under the Fourteenth Amendment of the Constitution, yet this protection may not be available much longer. The Constitution also provides that international treaties become the supreme law of the land, and child's rights advocates intend to use this provision to destroy family autonomy.

Citizens of the United Nations

On 16 February 1995, Madeleine Albright, U.S. ambassador to the UN, signed the United Nations Convention on the Rights of the Child, which was then forwarded to the Senate for ratification. Heralded as the ultimate solution to child abuse, this document is receiving enthusiastic support from Hillary Clinton. Assured that it simply reiterates our nation's resolve to protect children from abuse, a large number of senators have indicated their support for the document. Though ratification may take some time, supporters are determined to resurrect the treaty each year until it is ratified.

But this treaty does *not* protect children. The UN Convention, if ratified, would eliminate constitutional protection of the family and make all children in America "Wards of the State." Here's how:

Article 1 gives authority over the child to the state. Article 2 requires that every child be protected from punishment for his activities, expressed opinions, or because he has violated his parent's values. Proponents claim the treaty will eliminate corporal punishment. In fact, Great Britain, who has ratified the convention, is now being attacked by the UN for its failure to outlaw spanking.

Article 3 empowers the state to determine what is in the "best interest of the child" and to ensure that parents carry out their wishes. Articles 13 and 31 give children the right to full freedom of expression and access to all forms of art and entertainment. There is no exception for pornography.

The parent's ability to be involved in the religious training of their children is strictly curtailed by Article 14. If a child would rather watch cartoons than attend Sunday school, that is his prerogative, and parents cannot interfere. Nor could a parent object if the child becomes caught up in Satanism or other cult activities.

The right of children to freedom of association is guaranteed by Article 15. A parent is not allowed to restrict their children's companions or forbid gang involvement.

Article 16 gives children the right to privacy. If they wish to take their date to the bedroom, that's their business. State laws requiring parental notification of abortions would be eliminated. Parents could not enter a child's room without permission.

And, who will be responsible for teaching values? Article 17 has the answer: the mass media.

Considering the number of sexual encounters teenagers see on television each year, this idea is preposterous.

Other provisions in the treaty are equally alarming. Public outcry defeated federal health care, yet this treaty bypasses the will of the people by mandating socialized medicine (Article 24). Federally funded and operated child care, social security benefits for all children, and state control of all educational institutions is also required. The state is even empowered to determine the standard of living all homes should have and to ensure that all children be "brought up in the spirit of the ideals proclaimed in the Charter of the United Nations."

If a parent refuses to comply, Article 12 provides free legal representation to the child. Parents, of course, would have to pay for their own defense.

Children are already protected by law from abuse. Unfortunately, abuse still occurs because laws do not change the heart. It is ridiculous to think that a United Nations treaty can guarantee anyone a happy childhood. In fact, this treaty actually destroys a fundamental right of all children: the right to be raised in a loving home, free from bureaucratic interference.

11

Reclaiming Lost Ground

And when with the passage of time a nation's spiritual ideal is sapped, that nation falls, together with all its civil statutes and ideals.
—Dostoyevsky, *Diary of a Writer*

America's children are facing unprecedented challenges today, and drastic steps must be taken to ensure not only their future, but the future of our nation. As a society, we have lost our spiritual ideals. Government, which has grown steadily larger and more intrusive, cannot solve what ails the heart. Ultimately this is a battle that must be won in the community, on a one-to-one basis.

Changes do need to be made at the federal and state levels, however, to stop the policies which perpetuate these problems and to enable local communities to reclaim lost ground. This chapter will explore those policies and attitudes which, if incorporated, could help change the destructive paths so many American youth are taking.

Federal Changes

1. The current welfare system must be reformed. This is a topic which receives much lip service, but very little substance. Politicians, in their zeal to help the poor and capture votes, have created a self-perpetuating system that is destroying our work ethic and with it our inner cities. Women should not be paid to have children and keep the father out of the home. Sixteen-year-old girls should not be automatically offered a place to stay, food stamps, and a monthly check which increases with each illegitimate child.

When benefits are granted, they should be short-term and conditional, requiring work and/or education. Welfare must cease to be a way of life for able-bodied people. High school mothers should be required to continue in school and receive a diploma or GED. Training in viable job skills should also be given, and work requirements met. Much of the training these programs offer now is geared toward keeping women within the system. An example of this is the home health aide program. Recipients who go through this training quite often discover the only agency they are qualified to work for is social services. What single parents need is to learn skills that can command better than minimum wage.

2. Government should stop funding pornography via the National Endowment for the Arts. It is a matter of stewardship, not censorship, to set guidelines for how tax dollars are spent. Too often organizations such as these try to hide behind the First Amendment as they stick out their hands and demand money. This is ludicrous. Let "artists" such as Mapplethorpe compete in the open market, where

decent artists must work, and let the people vote with their dollars. With our deficit so high, it is unbelievable that Congress would think it necessary to spend taxpayers' dollars on photographs of a bullwhip sticking out of a man's rear end.[1]

3. Punitive taxes need to be reformed. This should not cause an excessive burden, since history shows that tax cuts stimulate the economy and increase revenues.

4. Congress needs to begin restoring a respect for the value of life in our nation by acknowledging the rights of unborn children.

5. Major reform is needed in the area of social services. The Federal Child Abuse Prevention and Treatment Act needs to be tossed out or drastically revised to protect the rights of children and families alike. Constitutional rights must be restored to families.

6. Congress must not ratify the United Nations Convention on the Rights of the Child. This international treaty would destroy family autonomy and strip parents of all authority over their families. The United Nations is not qualified to rear children.

7. Congress should take steps to protect the "free exercise" clause of the First Amendment which guarantees all citizens (including Christians) the right to free religious expression, whether or not they are on public property. Such expression should not be required of anyone, nor should it be prohibited.

8. Some of the resources currently going to cities for improvement projects should be used to restore an economic base in the inner cities. Experimental programs which have converted subsidized housing into privately owned property have been very successful in some areas. Emphasis should be put on making communities self-sufficient.

9. Goethe once observed, "What government is the best? That which teaches us to govern ourselves." The federal government needs to stop meddling in education and other areas over which it does not have authority. The move to create a national school board and laws which mandate Outcome Based Education are clear violations of the Constitution. These powers belong to the state.

State and Local Reforms

State and local governments are more intimately touched by the problems of youth violence, ballooning welfare roles, and crumbling inner cities. Even so, no government bureaucracy is capable of resolving these problems, but there are policies which, if adopted, could help strengthen families and communities.

1. Education is a key for empowering young people to break free from an ongoing cycle of generational poverty. For many students, however, school is a frustrating experience because they cannot read proficiently. Educators persist in using whole language to the exclusion of phonics, and the result is dismal failure. Versions of this method have been tried and have failed numerous times over the last century. Local communities should respond to parents' concerns in this area and restore phonics. Promoters of the look-say method brag that a student should be able to read 1,554 words by the end of fourth grade. They don't tell parents that students taught phonics will be able to read and understand 24,000 words by that time.[2] The bottom line is this: parents should have the final authority over their children's education.

In addition, teachers should be required to meet standards of proficiency and should be judged on performance. There are many excellent teachers in our public schools, but many do not meet the competency levels we would expect of a high school graduate.[3]

Some states, such as Colorado, have mandated Outcome Based Education in an effort to dictate educational philosophy and usurped parental control from the process. This is not in the best interest of the students or community.

Local governments should allow open enrollment, which would ensure parental choice and force schools to compete for students. This free-market approach would result in better quality, just as it does in industry. A voucher program granting free choice among public schools would allow parents an opportunity to pick an environment which meets the needs of their children and would empower them to demand and receive better quality. When Chicago, which has had some of the most dismal school ratings, enacted a voucher program, one particularly poor school was finally forced to respond to parents' complaints. On the first day of school, the only ones to arrive were the teachers. Needless to say, the community finally got someone to listen.

Most of our schools are geared toward college preparation, not job market skills, even though many students have no intention of pursuing a degree. Offering a variety of choices, including trade schools, could offer some students much needed motivation to finish their education, and give them a marketable skill to take into the job market.

Funding for these programs would be available by trimming down administrative staff. In some areas the ratio of administrators to teachers is one to three, while the ratio of teacher to students is one to thirty or thirty-five. This points to a definite lack of priority.

2. States should not mandate sex education. This is a prerogative of the parents. Sex education has been shown to fail, and the younger the students are when they enroll, the greater their chances are of becoming sexually active at a young age. Parents in the community should be allowed to determine if they want this training in schools and should be allowed to choose the curriculum. Programs which promote unhealthy, promiscuous behavior should not be funded. Abstinence programs should be encouraged and not rejected under the ridiculous assertion that such programs are religious.

3. Reform of state and social service agencies is essential to protect children without destroying healthy families. Records should be opened for review, children should only be removed when they are in imminent danger, and family preservation should be a priority.

Community Involvement

Next to the family, the community can be the most effective tool for affecting change. Unfortunately, this is an almost untapped resource, partly because it is dependent upon individual efforts, and partly because many communities lack resources to affect the changes they would like to make. But, collective, grass-roots efforts can be highly effective.

Influencing the Media

The media has a strong impact on behavior and is an area that should be targeted for action. The entertainment industry is a business and depends upon community support. Neighbors can ban together and demand a quality product. The first step is to approach the radio or television station or network and in a reasoned manner with concern. In some cases, this can be effective. There are media who respond to community concerns. For example, some black stations such as WBLS-FM in New York and KACE-FM in Los Angeles have stopped airing music which degrades women and glorifies violence, sex, and drugs.[4]

If the media is unresponsive to complaints and suggestions, the next approach would be to contact sponsors and eventually organize boycotts.

Rebuilding the Black Community

Another key to resolving problems is for community leaders to stop blaming society for their circumstances and to take responsibility for change. The past cannot be changed, and continuing to focus on old injustices only creates hatred and hopelessness. This is especially true for the black community in the inner city. As William Raspberry writes: "Rights, even when widely distributed and fairly enforced, have not solved our problems. . . . Unfortunately we have spent more time teaching our children about the world's unfairness than about its general tendency to reward effort."[5]

America's history in relation to blacks has not been good, but this generation cannot compensate for sins of the past. What we need to do now is go forward. When leaders in minority communities persist in perpetuating a spirit of victimization, when they continually preach that the circumstances their constituency finds themselves in is beyond their control, they are destroying the spirit and hope that is needed for people to overcome inequities and improve their lives and communities.

Dr. Louis Sullivan is a product of a poor black neighborhood who became a medical doctor and served as president of Morehouse University and secretary of Health and Human Services. Yet, he tells young people that they must accept full responsibility for their own behavior. In an address before the Fourth Annual Conference on the Black Male, Sullivan admonished his audience to stop taking drugs, getting drunk, and fathering illegitimate children. They were responsible for their own success and failure, he insisted, and the black community must return to the values that had strengthened it in the past.

> The black community was able to endure two hundred years of slavery and more than eighty years of segregation. Why? Because we maintained that sense of community and connectedness with one another. Even in the wake of slavery, intact families were the norm in the black community, not the exception as they are today. . . . In many respects, we survived better as a people back then. And it is time to remember what worked in our own social structure. . . .

> Solutions to the problems of the black community will be found within the black community. We must transform a culture of violence, which defeats and destroys, into a culture of character, which uplifts and empowers. We need strong families—families that spend time together.[6]

Battling Gangs

Kids join gangs for a variety of reasons, but mainly because of dysfunctional families and no sense of options. Their value systems are morally bankrupt. The most successful people in the neighborhood are drug dealers. The leading cause of death for young males in gang-infested neighborhoods is homicide, and most boys don't expect to live beyond twenty-five years of age. With no sense of future and no apparent options, kids give up on life and on themselves.

In order for a program to have any success dealing with gang members, they must help provide options, to help members see value in altering their lifestyle. It is pointless to tell a gang member to clean up his act and go to school if there are no jobs.

Values cannot be taught without dealing with the spiritual condition. Those programs which have been most effective in helping youth leave gangs teach goal-setting, job skills, help young people find employment, and model sincere, spiritual values.

Prevention: The Best Cure

The key to battling gangs is prevention. Many kids who have been caught up in a gang do not live long enough to change or become so hardened that they seem unreachable. But, children who become involved in prevention at a very young age stand a much better chance of survival. These programs must address the causes of gang involvement and target academics and skill development. But, no social program can be successful without a spiritual emphasis. This is the premise upon which John Perkins of Pasadena, California, started the Christian Community Development Association, which now has over 350 organizations and 3,000 members.

Neighborhood Ministries in Denver, Colorado, is one of these organizations. Neighborhood Minis-

tries was founded by Ted Travis in 1980. After growing up in New York, Ted had managed to escape
his poverty-stricken neighborhood to study music in
Vienna, Austria. It was there that he became a
Christian. In spite of his vows to never return to a
community like he had grown up in, he began to
have a burden for inner-city youth. The result was
Neighborhood Ministries.

The program focuses on youth development and
is based on a belief that you cannot separate the
social from the spiritual, that discipleship involves
the complete person. It is not enough to preach
good values, you must model those beliefs. The
majority of the children in the surrounding area
come from single-parent homes which lack male
role models, discipline, and financial resources. The
ministry tries to address those needs.

Programs involve not just the youth, but the
whole family, beginning with a Mothers of
Preschoolers (MOPS) program, where spiritual values and practical parenting skills are taught. Classes
and clubs are held for all school age children. These
include education, tutoring, a learning center, literacy development, music groups, and the Harambee
youth clubs. In addition to music, the clubs offer
Bible studies, rap sessions, monthly recreational
activities, camps and retreats, and a six week summer day camp.

Currently, the ministry is hoping to bring busi-
nessmen in from outlying communities to teach the
local community how to rebuild a business base in
their community. In a neighborhood where the most
profitable business is the drug trade, there is a
desperate need to offer alternatives.

The success of these programs, Travis says, is
based upon building a dream in young people who

are surrounded by hopelessness and developing self-esteem in each child by helping them see themselves as a unique creation of God.

Call to the Church

The Christian doctrine is a doctrine of reconciliation: first, a reconciliation of man to his Creator, and then of man to man. Because of this, the Church is uniquely qualified to reach the youth of all communities. It is incumbent on us to cross racial, cultural, and financial barriers to affect a change in our community.

Organizations interested in programs such as Neighborhood Ministries may write:

Neighborhood Ministries
2323 Emerson Street
Denver, CO 80205

12

Winning at Home

There is no guaranteed formula for raising perfect kids. If there was, we would all be missing the first ingredient: perfect parents. Every person is ultimately responsible for his own actions, and teens from the best families can make destructive choices.

Yet, family is still the most effective tool for combating temptations and influences young people face today. Children from strong, loving, disciplined homes rarely join gangs or attempt suicide. The family was the first social institution ever created, and it is the most powerful. The problems our children face are basically the result of two things: first, the abandonment of godly values; and second, the breakdown of the family.

Teaching Values

Parents are ultimately responsible for a child's academic, moral, social, and spiritual education. And, if we don't train them, society will. Values are not somehow passed through the genes or gleaned through osmosis: they are taught daily, by example and by developing a strong, supportive, and open relationship with children.

Because of the fast pace most families are on, there is a tendency to believe that kids need "quality time" more than "quantity time." That's not true. They need both, but unfortunately most teens do not get either. A recent study of adolescent-parent relationships revealed that more than half of the teens involved " 'spend less than thirty minutes a day with their fathers; and 44 percent spend less than thirty minutes with their mothers'. . . . Even more alarming, 'one-fourth of the ninth graders in this study spend less than five minutes (in an average day) alone with father to talk, play, or just be together.' " This was not referring to quality time spent one-on-one with the parents; it was referring to the amount of time they spent in the same room. Most adults spend more time reading the paper and watching the news than they do with their children during the most crucial years of their lives.[1]

Considering the lack of interaction between parents and their children, it's not difficult to understand why they are so easily influenced by schools, the media, and peers. Josh McDowell and his "Why Wait?" ministry has found that the number one thing kids are seeking is intimacy, to feel loved and cherished by someone. Even those from good homes express a yearning to share time with their parents, to be hugged and valued and heard. When they can't find that with parents, they look elsewhere.

The importance of time together (real time, not watching television in the same room) is supported by a mountain of empirical data. Children who have close, open communication with their parents are less likely to become sexually involved as teen-agers. Recent studies have shown that families who eat thirty-minute meals together at least three times a week are less likely to take drugs or become involved in gangs or delinquent activities.[2] The following are techniques for building families and reaching young people in the family and community.

Taking Time

1. Turn off the TV. While television can be beneficial, it is the greatest time-thief ever created. When parents are glued to the TV, they cannot listen to their kids.

2. Plan several evening meals together as a family—and keep the television off. This is a great opportunity to discover what is going on in a child's life.

3. Plan one evening each week as a family night. Children seem to always be on the go, with sports, school activities, and "hanging out" with friends. Plan your calendars in advance, and then make the evening a priority. If a parent makes plans to do something with a child and then forgets or reneges because of other conflicts, the child is deeply hurt. To a child this means, "You are not important."

4. Practice what you preach. If you want them to be substance free, then you must be. Kids whose parents use marijuana are more likely to join gangs and use harder drugs. Parents who watch nudity and promiscuity on television make it difficult for teens to remain chaste. Live the standards you want them to emulate.

5. Listen. When you actively listen to your children, you are telling them "You are important and worthwhile."

6. Maintain consistency. Set the rules and standards, and stick by them. This does not mean that a parent should be a dictator, imperiously handing down commands and expecting blind obedience. Explain the rules and your reasons for them, then

insist on obedience. It is important for your child to understand the values and reasoning behind your decisions. It won't be long before he will be making decisions on his own. A college student needs to have better justification that "Mom and Dad said so" when he is confronted with a potentially damaging temptation.

Once the boundaries have been set, then they must be consistently upheld. A child should be told ahead of time what the consequences for disobedience will be, and then they should be lovingly enforced.

7. Be willing to say, "I'm sorry." Kids are usually quick to forgive if asked.

8. Teach your children deferred gratification and goal-setting. Kids who believe in a future are less likely to be involved in destructive behavior.

Helping Kids Handle Sex

Talk to your kids about sex. Do not leave this up to the schools. If your children are in public school, make it very clear that you want to know in advance when they are having sex ed. Some grade schools are starting in kindergarten, which is much too young. Children that young are not emotionally mature enough for that knowledge, and statistics indicate that knowing too much, too soon promotes promiscuous and potentially harmful behavior. If your child is not ready, don't have him in school that day.

If you develop and maintain open communication with your children they will begin to ask questions about their sexuality, where babies come from, etc., as they are ready. Only give them as much information as they seem to want at the time. If you handle the questions naturally and without embarrassment, they will continue to ask as they become prepared for more knowledge. There are several excellent books for children at Christian bookstores which handle some of the early questions very well.

As a child matures, you need to be very honest and frank about the purpose of sex and the emotional and physical consequences of premarital relationships. Give them suggestions on how to respond to pressure. Help them avoid dangerous settings, i.e., too much time alone with dates. Encourage group activities; let them bring dates to family outings, and take them in groups to activities. Get to know your children's friends.

Encourage your children to join a chastity pledge group. Use peer pressure to your advantage. These groups offer kids a support base as well as practical skills for surviving in a promiscuous world.

Your Kids and the Media

Your children are affected by what they read, see, and hear. The first step is for parents to take an inventory of their own habits. Do the movies they watch and the music they hear convey the lifestyle and values they wish their children to emulate? Parents need to set the pace.

The message does count. Set standards in your home and explain why. If something inappropriate does pop up, discuss it with your children. Let them help to analyze what they have seen. Listen to their music. If your children already have tapes with negative messages, listen to the music together, and explain why you are setting the standards. Offer a buy-back policy, where you will replace their substandard tapes with positive ones that meet their tastes. Be reasonable, but remember, you are in charge.

Your Family and the Schools

The religion being taught in public schools today is humanism. Even though there are many fine teachers, the textbooks and course content are slanted to undermine traditional Judeo-Christian standards. Many families have opted for private or home schools where they can assure that their children are receiving a quality education. Both are excellent options. Homeschooling, in particular, has been gaining a great deal of popularity in both the Christian and secular communities. Studies take less time, families have more quality time together, and the students receive excellent academic attention. Homeschoolers score consistently in the top 15 percent in college placement tests and are actively recruited by Ivy League schools.

If you choose to have your children in public schools, then it is imperative that you remain actively involved in their education. Find out what they are studying, get to know their teachers, discuss course content that conflicts with your values. Even parents who do not have children in public schools should attempt to influence the local public schools in a positive way. The majority of our nation's children will be educated in the public setting, and it is imperative that we take an interest. After all, we pay for it.

Reaching Out

A parent's first priority must be their own family, but we cannot stop there. Too many children do not have stable home lives. We are all part of a greater community, and what happens in the inner city does effect what happens in the suburbs. Christians, in particular, should be involved in reaching out to families and young people in need.

The following are suggestions for making a difference in your community:

1. Adopt a single-parent family. Building a friendship can offer many avenues of ministry. Your family can provide a role model for the missing parent. You can help in practical ways with car maintenance, parenting skills, budgeting advice, job hunting skills, and friendship.

2. Share resources with inner-city community programs, both financial and personal. Many of these are in desperate need of tutors, coaches, teachers, counselors, etc.

3. Be active in your schools.

4. Involve your family in a community outreach.

5. Be informed. Samuel Johnson once wrote, "Ignorance, when voluntary, is criminal."

Notes

Chapter One

1. Charles Colson, *Against the Night: Living in the New Dark Ages* (Ann Arbor, Mich: Servant Publications, 1989), 79–80.

2. Josh McDowell, with Bob Hostetler, "Help Your Teen Make the Right Choice," *Focus on the Family* (November 1994): 3.

3. Ibid.

4. Ibid., 4.

5. Barbara Hattemer and Robert Showers, *Don't Touch That Dial* (Lafayette, La.: Huntington House Publishers, 1993), 31.

6. Alexis de Tocqueville, *Democracy in America*, trans. by Henry Reeve (New York: Alfred A. Knopf, 1945), 295–307.

7. Ibid., 303–307.

8. Colson, 28–29.

9. Christopher J. Klicka, *Homeschooling: The Right Choice* (Gresham, Oreg.: Noble Publishing, 1993), 78.

10. Ibid., 11.

11. Ibid., 78–79.

12. Tim LaHaye, *The Battle for the Mind* (Old Tappan, N.J.: Fleming H. Revell, 1980), 27.

13. Klicka, *Homeschooling*, 80.

14. LaHaye, *The Battle*, 44.

15. Sally D. Reed, *NEA: Propaganda Front of the Radical Left* (Washington, D.C.: National Council for Better Education, 1984), 57.

16. Klicka, *Homeschooling*, 87.

17. Peter Collier and David Horowitz, *Destructive Generation: Second Thoughts about the Sixties* (New York: Summit Books, 1989), 15.

18. Ibid., 335.

19. Tocqueville, *Democracy in America*, 307.

20. Colson, *Against the Night*, 80.

Chapter Two

1. Josh McDowell and Dick Day, *Why Wait: What You Need to Know about the Teen Sexuality Crisis* (Nashville: Thomas Nelson Publishers, 1987), 24.

2. Joy Overbeck, "Sex Too Soon," *Parents Magazine* (September 1994): 42.

3. Elizabeth Gleich, et. al., "Too Soon, Too Sorry," *People Weekly* (24 October 1994): 52.

4. Joseph P. Shapiro, "Teenage Sex: Just Say Wait," *U.S. News and World Report* (26 July 1993): 2.

5. McDowell, *Why Wait*, 22.

6. Ibid., 23–24.

7. Ibid.

8. Ibid., 24.

9. Ibid.

10. Gleick, "Too Soon," 50.

11. Ibid., 44.

12. Ibid., 45.

13. Bill Scanlon, "Pregnancies perpetuate poverty cycle," *Rocky Mountain News* (31 October 1993): 20A.

14. Bill Scanlon, "Poor girls, boyfriends welcome babies," *Rocky Mountain News* (31 October 1993): 21A.

15. Bill Scanlon, "15-year-old mom finds few regrets in new role," *Rocky Mountain News* (31 October 1993): 20A.

16. Bill Scanlon, "Pregnancies perpetuate poverty," 20A.

17. McDowell, *Why Wait*, 47.

18. Bill Scanlon, "15-year-old mom finds few regrets in new role," 20A.

19. Mona Charen, "Abortion Risk No Longer Deniable," *Rocky Mountain News* (20 October 1994): 54A.

20. Ibid.

21. Ibid.

22. McDowell, *Why Wait*, 48.

23. Marjorie Little, *Sexually Transmitted Diseases* (New York: Chelsea House Publishers, 1991), 82.

24. Michael Broadman, et.al., *Straight Talk about Sexually Transmitted Diseases* (New York: Facts on File, 1993), 61.

25. Josh McDowell, "Sex, Lies and Truth," (Waco, TX: Word, 1988), video.

26. Associated Press, "Many in U.S. naive about sex, poll says," *Rocky Mountain News* (14 February 1995): 20A.

27. Josh McDowell, "Myths About Teenage Sexuality," (Waco, TX: Word, 1988), video.

28. Broadman, *Straight Talk*, 46.

29. Ibid., 62.

30. McDowell, *Why Wait*, 16.

31. Donald D. Schroeder, "AIDS Proves Sexual Liberation is Harmful," in *Sexual Values: Opposing Viewpoints* (San Diego: Greenhaven Press, 1993), 40

32. Broadman, 66.

33. Ibid., 69.

34. McDowell, *Why Wait*, 48.

35. Rae Lewis-Thronton, "Facing AIDS," *Essence* (December 1994): 63.

36. Broadman, *Straight Talk*, 82.

37. Michael Thomas Ford, *100 Questions and Answers about AIDS: A Guide for Young People* (New York: New Discovery Books, 1992), 37.

38. Josh McDowell, "Where Youth are Today: What You Should Know About the Teen Sex Crisis," (Waco, TX: Word, 1988), video.

39. Ibid.

Chapter Three

1. John C. Ensslin, "Six Littleton teens die trying to beat train," *Rocky Mountain News* (9 April 1995): 4A.

2. Stephen Arterburn and Jim Burns, *Drug-Proof Your Kids* (Pamona, Calif.: Focus on the Family, 1989), 12.

3. Ibid.

4. Ibid., 15.

5. Christopher J. Klicka, *Homeschooling: The Right Choice* (Gersham, Oreg.: Noble Publishing Associates, 1993), 54.

6. Arterburn, *Drug-Proof*, 11–12.

7. Antonio Black, "The Drugging of America's Children," *Redbook* (December 1994): 42.

8. Ibid.

9. Ibid., 44.

10. Ibid.

11. Ibid., 42.

12. Ibid., 44.

13. Arterburn and Burns, 11–12.

14. Ibid.

15. Associated Press, "Marijuana use by 8th-graders doubles since '91, survey says," *Rocky Mountain News* (Denver, CO) (13 December 1994): 3A.

16. Ibid.

17. Arterburn and Burns, 22.

18. Mary Rose McGeady, *Am I Going to Heaven?* (New York: Covenant House): 28.

19. Michelle Ingrassia, "America's Runaways," *Newsweek* (4 April 1994): 64–65.

20. Ibid.

21. Ibid.

22. Brenda Scott, *Out of Control: Who's Watching Our Child Protection Agencies?* (Lafayette, LA: Huntington House, 1994): 106.

23. McGeady, *Am I Going to Heaven?*: 16–17.

24. Ozzy Osbourne, "Suicide Solution," song quoted in *Learn to Discern* by Robert G. DeMoss, Jr., (Grand Rapids, MI: Zondervan, 1992): 79.

25. Ibid.

26. Josh McDowell and Dick Day, *Why Wait? What You Need to Know About the Teen Sexuality Crisis* (Nashville: Thomas Nelson Publishers, 1987): 30–31.

27. Ibid., 31.

28. Hubert Buchsbaum, "The American Teenager," *Scholastic Update* (14 January 1994): 9.

Chapter Four

1. Steven Manning, "A National Emergency," *Scholastic Update* (5 April 1991): 2.

2. Barbara Kantrowitz, "Wild in the Streets," *Newsweek* (2 August 1993): 40.

3. Manning, "A National Emergency," 2–3.

4. Kantrowitz, "Wild in the Streets," 40.

5. Jon D. Hall, "A Boy and His Son," *Time* (2 August 1993): 20.

6. Ibid.

7. Kantrowitz, "Wild in the Streets," 40.

8. Ronald Henkoy, "Kids are Killing, Dying, Bleeding," *Fortune* (10 August 1992): 6A.

9. Jon D. Hall, "A Boy and His Son," 20.

10. Christopher J. Klicka, *Homeschooling: The Right Choice* (Gresham, Oreg.: Noble Publishing Associates, 1993), 50.

11. Steven Manning, "Stop the Violence," *Scholastic Update* (11 February 1994), 2.

12. Sandra Arbetter, "Violence, a Growing Threat," *Current Health* (February 1993): 9.

13. Klicka, *Homeschooling*, 53.

14. Ibid.

15. Kantrowitz, "Wild in the Streets," 40.

16. Phil Sudo, "What Kind of Justice," *Scholastic Update* (5 April 1991): 10.

17. "A Young Man with a Taste for Stabbing," *Newsweek* (15 August 1994): 24.

18. Leslie Faust, "The Ultimate Price," *Scholastic Update* (5 April 1991): 13

19. Michael Marriott, "Living in 'Lockdown,'" *Newsweek* (23 January 1995): 56.

20. Karen N. Peart, "Lessons in Survival," *Scholastic Update* (11 February 1994): 16.

21. Jerry Adler, "Growing Up Scared," *Newsweek* (10 January 1994): 44.

Chapter Five

1. John McCormick, with Peter Annin, "Death of a Child Criminal," *Newsweek* (12 September 94): 45.

2. Julie Grace, "There are no Children Here," *Time* (12 September 1994): 44.

3. John McCormick, "Death of a Child Criminal," 45.

4. Ibid.

5. Karen Osman, *Gangs* (San Diego: Lucent Books, Inc., 1992): 13.

6. Ibid, 17.

7. Ibid., 24.

8. Ibid., 30–31.

9. James Earl Hardy, "Violent Youth," *Scholastic Update* (5 April 1991): 6.

10. Osman, *Gangs*, 25.

11. Allison Abner, "gangsta girls," *Essence* (July 1994): 66.

12. Connie Leslie, "Girls will be Girls," *Newsweek* (2 August 1993): 44.

13. Gina Sikes, "Girls in the Hood," *Scholastic Update* (11 February 1994): 21.

14. Leslie, "Girls will be Girls," 44.

15. Sikes, "Girls in the Hood," 21.

16. Ibid., 20.

17. Ibid.

18. Daniel Ames Carrie, *Street Gangs* (Portland, Oreg.: Pocket Press, Inc., 1993), 53–54.

19. Ibid., 54.

20. Ibid.

21. Margot Webb, *Coping with Street Gangs* (New York: The Rosen Publishing Group, 1992), 31.

22. Sikes, "Girls in the Hood," 22.

23. Sandra Arbetter, "Violence, A Growing Threat," *Current Health* (February 1994): 11.

24. Sikes, "Girls in the Hood," 22.

25. Ibid.

26. "Adolescents and Children Injured or Killed in Drive-by Shootings in Los Angeles," *New England Journal of Medicine* (3 February 1994): 3.

27. Webb, *Coping with Street Gangs*, 31.

28. Ibid., 58.

29. Ibid., 57.

30. Ibid.

31. Abner, "gangsta girls," 65, 177.

Chapter Six

1. Michele Ingrassia, "Life Ain't Nothing," *Newsweek* (19 July 1993): 16.

2. Ibid., 17.

3. Dr. Reed Bell, with Frank York, *Prescription Death* (Lafayette, La.: Huntington House, 1993), 25.

4. Ibid., 26.

5. Raymond Vaulo, "Living Wills Can Lead to Unnecessary Deaths," in *Death and Dying: Opposing Viewpoints* edited by Janelle Rohr (San Diego: Greenhaven Press, 1993), 83.

6. Joyce Schofield, M.D., "Euthanasia is Unethical," in *Euthanasia: Opposing Viewpoints* edited by Neal Bernards (San Diego: Greenhaven Press, 1993), 25–26.

7. Nat Hentoff, "Doctors Should Oppose Euthanasia Decisions" in *Euthanasia: Opposing Viewpoints* edited by Neal Bernards (San Diego: Greenhaven Press, 1993), 98.

8. Bell, *Prescription Death*, 82.

9. Susan Neuburt Terkel, *Abortion: Facing the Issues* (New York: Franklin Watts, 1988), 21.

10. Ibid., 69.

11. Bell, *Prescription Death*, 79.

12. Ibid., 101.

13. Ibid., 101–102.

14. "Focus on the Family" broadcast (15 April 1995).

15. Thomas and Celia Scully, "Playing God" in *Euthanasia: Opposing Viewpoints* edited by Neal Bernards (San Diego: Greenhaven Press, 1993), 209.

16. E. Fritz Schmerl, "The Right to Die is Ethical," in *Euthanasia: Opposing Viewpoints* edited by Neal Bernards (San Diego: Greenhaven Press, 1993), 45–46.

17. Earl Shelp, "Active Infant Euthanasia is Acceptable," in *Euthanasia: Opposing Viewpoints* edited by Neal Bernards (San Diego: Greenhaven Press, 1993), 190.

18. Ibid., 120.

19. H. Tristan Engelhardt, Jr., "The Foundation of Bioethics" in *Euthanasia: Opposing Viewpoints* edited by Neal Bernards (San Diego: Greenhaven Press, 1993), 192.

20. Howard Caplon, "Doctors Should Support Euthanasia Decisions," in *Euthanasia: Opposing Viewpoints* edited by Neal Bernards (San Diego: Greenhaven, 1993), 90.

21. Gerald A. Larue, "Patients Should Decide," in *Euthanasia: Opposing Viewpoints* edited by Neal Bernards (San Diego: Greenhaven Press, 1993), 153.

22. C. Everett Koop, M.D. and Timothy Johnson, M.D., *Let's Talk* (Grand Rapids, Mich.: Zondervan, 1992), 39.

23. Bell, *Prescription Death*, 103.

24. Associated Press, "Oregon will vote on suicide measure," *Rocky Mountain News* (15 October 1994): 50A.

25. Richard Fenigsen, M.D., "Euthanasia: the Medicine of Fear and Death," in *Euthanasia: Opposing Viewpoints* edited by Neal Bernards (San Diego: Greenhaven Press, 1993), 80–81.

26. Christopher Boyd, "Murder in Miami," *Scholastic Update* (11 February 1993): 8.

Chapter Seven

1. Robert Edwin Herzstein, *The Nazis* (Alexandria, Va.: Time-Life Books, 1980), 128.

2. Ibid.

3. Ibid., 91.

4. Christopher J. Klicka, *Homeschooling: The Right Choice* (Gresham, Oreg.: Noble Publishing Associates, 1993), 115.

5. Ibid.

6. George Geiger, *John Dewey in Perspective* (New York: McGraw-Hill Books, 1958), 89.

7. Sally Reed, *NEA: Propaganda Front of the Radical Left* (Washington, D.C.: National Council for Better Education), 6–7.

8. Ibid., 70.

9. Ibid., 11.

10. Ibid., 14.

11. Berny Morson, "Education 'reforms' questioned," *Rocky Mountain News* (6 November 1993): 12A.

12. Berny Morson, "Nation is Watching Littleton Schools," *Rocky Mountain News* (7 November 1993): 35A.

13. Berny Morson, "Back-to-basics battle at polls," *Rocky Mountain News* (31 December 1993): 30A.

14. Dave Schiflett, "Littleton school board race becomes slathered in sleaze," *Rocky Mountain News* (16 October 1993): 56A.

15. Ibid.

16. Betty Miles, *Save the Earth: An Action Handbook for Kids* (New York: Alfred A. Knopf, 1991), ix.

17. Ibid., ix–x.

18. Charles Krauthammer, "Hiroshima, Mon Petit," *Time* (27 March 1995): 80.

19. Toshi Maruki, *Hiroshima No Pika* (New York: Lothrop, Lee and Shepard Books, 1980), 192.

20. Krauthammer, "Hiroshima, Mon Petit," 80.

Chapter Eight

1. James M. Arata, "Sex Education Should Focus on Morality," in *Sexual Values: Opposing Viewpoints* Lisa Orr, ed., (San Diego: Greenhaven Press, 1993), 113.

2. Dana Mack, "What Sex Educators Teach," *Commentary* (August 1993): 33.

3. Celeste McGovern, "Too Much, Too Soon," *Alberta Report* (14 March 1994): 28.

4. Ibid., 33.

5. Ibid.

6. Faye Wattleton, "Sex Educators Should Not Focus on Morality," in *Sexual Values: Opposing Viewpoints* Lisa Orr, ed., (San Diego: Greenhaven Press, 1993), 119.

7. McGovern, "Too Much, Too Soon," 28.

8. Ibid.

9. Loren E. Acher, Ph.D., et. al., *AIDS-Proofing Your Kids* (Hillsboro, Oreg.: Beyond Words Publishing, 1992), 70–71.

10. Ibid., 95.

11. Ellen Hopkins, "What Kids Really Learn in Sex Ed," *Parents* (September 1993): 46.

12. McGovern, "Too Much, Too Soon," 28.

13. Ibid.

14. Josh McDowell, "Sex, Lies and Truth," (Waco, TX: Word, 1986), video.

15. Ibid.

16. Thomas Sowell, "A Dangerous Myth," in *Sexual Values: Opposing Viewpoints* Lisa Orr, ed., (San Diego: Greenhaven Press, 1993), 114.

17. Arata, "Sex Education Should Focus on Morality," 114.

18. Ibid., 34.

19. McGovern, "Too Much, Too Soon," 28.

20. Ibid.

21. Hopkins, "What Kids Really Learn," 46.

22. Ibid.

23. Ibid.

Chapter Nine

1. Michael Medved, *Hollywood vs. America* (New York: HarperCollins Zondervan, 1992), 30.

2. Ibid.

3. Ibid., 4.

4. Alan Dumas, "Comedy Scrubs Up," *Rocky Mountain News* (19 March 1995): 62–63A.

5. Ibid., 62.

6. Medved, *Hollywood vs. America*, 28.

7. Josh McDowell and Dick Day, *Why Wait?* (Nashville: Thomas Nelson, 1987), 45.

8. Ibid., 46.

9. Loren E. Acher, Ph.D., et. al., "Murder She Saw," *Scholastic Update* (11 February 1994): 12.

10. Ibid., 13.

11. Robert G. DeMoss, Jr., *Learn to Discern* (Grand Rapids, Mich.: Zondervan, 1992), 78.

12. Medved, *Hollywood vs. America*, 101.

13. DeMoss, Jr., *Learn to Discern*, 68.

14. Medved, *Hollywood vs. America*, 197.

15. Ibid., 196.

16. Barbara Hattemer and H. Robert Showers, *Don't Touch That Dial* (Lafayette, La.: Huntington House Publishers), 127.

17. Ibid., 128.

18. Ibid.

19. Ibid., 130.

20. Medved, *Hollywood vs. America*, 199.

21. Nathan McCall, "My Rap Against Rap," *Reader's Digest* (May 1994): 64–65.

22. Ibid., 65.

23. Ibid.

24. Ibid.

25. Dana Rohrabacher, address before the U.S. House of Representatives (13 September 1989).

26. Medved, *Hollywood vs. America*, 26.

27. Ibid., 27.

Chapter Ten

1. Alexis de Tocqueville, *Democracy in America*, trans. Henry Reeve (New York: Alfred A. Knopf, 1945), 304.

2. Barbara Dafoe Whitehead, "Dan Quayle Was Right," *Atlantic Monthly* (April 1993): 50.

3. Ibid, 52.

4. Charles Colson, *Against the Night: Living in the New Dark Ages* (Ann Arbor, Mich.: Servant Publications, 1989), 73.

5. Whitehead, "Dan Quayle Was Right," 52.

6. Ibid., 60.

7. Jerry Adler, "Growing Up Scared," *Newsweek* (10 January 1994): 44.

8. Michael Medved, *Hollywood vs. America* (New York: HarperCollins Zondervan, 1992), 110.

9. Whitehead, "Dan Quayle Was Right," 55.

10. Ibid.

11. Brenda Scott, *Out of Control: Who's Watching Our Child Protection Services?* (Lafayette, La.: Huntington House Publishers, 1994), 45.

12. Josh McDowell, with Dick Day, *Why Wait?* (Nashville: Thomas Nelson Publishers, 1987), 65.

13. Barbara Dafoe Whitehead, "Rethinking Divorce's Impact on Children," *Rocky Mountain News* (Denver, CO: 5 August 1993): 3D.

14. Whitehead, "Dan Quayle was Right," 60–62.

15. Ibid., 62.

16. Ibid.

17. Ibid.

18. Ken Magid and Carole A. McKelvey, *High Risk: Children Without a Conscious* (New York: Bantam Books, 1987), 169.

19. Elizabeth Gleick, et.al., "The Baby Trap," *People Weekly* (24 October 1994): 28.

20. Ken Silverstein, "Can We Reform Welfare," *Scholastic Update* (10 March 1995), 15.

21. Adler, "Growing Up Scared," 44.

22. Magid, *High Risk*, 186–187.

23. Whitehead, "Dan Quayle Was Right," 65.

24. McDowell, *Why Wait?*, 60.

25. Ibid.

26. Ibid.

27. Ibid, 25.

28. Magid, *High Risk*, 111.

29. Bill Scanlon, "Birthrate Fueling Crime?" *Rocky Mountain News* (31 October 1993): 21A.

30. Ibid., 112.

31. Ibid., 133.

32. Ibid., 121.

33. Ibid., 128.

34. Charles Colson and Jack Eckerd, *Why America Doesn't Work* (Dallas: Word Publishing, 1991), 76.

35. William Bennett, *The De-Valuing of America* (New York: Summit Books, 1992), 188.

36. Ibid, 192.

37. Ibid.

38. "The New Realism," *US News and World Report* (25 May 1992): 94.

39. Colson, *Why America Doesn't Work*, 74–75.

40. Ibid., 76.

41. Ibid.

Chapter Eleven

1. "The National Endowment for the Arts Should Be Defunded," *Sexual Values: Opposing Viewpoints* edited by Lisa Orr (San Diego: Greenhaven Press, 1993), 170.

2. Christopher Klicka, *Homeschooling: The Right Choice* (Gresham, Oreg.: Noble Publishing, 1993), 33.

3. Ibid., 31.

4. Nathan McCall, "My Rap Against Rap," *Reader's Digest* (May 1994): 66.

5. Charles Colson and Jack Eckerd, *Why America Doesn't Work* (Dallas: Word Publishing, 1991), 89.

6. Ibid., 87.

Chapter Twelve

1. Josh McDowell and Dick Day, *Why Wait?* (Nashville: Thomas Nelson, 1987), 61.

2. Allison Abner, "gangsta girls," *Essence* (July 1994): 188.

We welcome comments from our readers. Feel free to write to us at the following address:

Editorial Department
Huntington House Publishers
P.O. Box 53788
Lafayette, LA 70505

More Good Books from Huntington House

Out of Control—
Who's Watching Our Child
Protection Agencies?
by Brenda Scott

This book of horror stories is true. The deplorable and unauthorized might of Child Protection Services is capable of reaching into and destroying any home in America. No matter how innocent and happy your family may be, you are one accusation away from disaster. Social workers are allowed to violate constitutional rights and often become judge, jury, and executioner. Innocent parents may appear on computer registers and be branded "child abuser" for life. Every year, it is estimated that over 1 million people are falsely accused of child abuse in this country. You could be next, says author and speaker Brenda Scott.

ISBN 1-56384-069-3 $9.99

Political Correctness:
The Cloning of the American Mind
by David Thibodaux, Ph.D.

The author, a professor of literature at the University of Southwestern Louisiana, confronts head on the movement that is now being called Political Correctness. Political correctness, says Thibodaux, "is an umbrella under which advocates of civil rights, gay and lesbian rights, feminism, and environmental causes have gathered." To incur the wrath of these groups, one only has to disagree with them on political, moral, or social issues. To express traditionally Western concepts in universities today can result in not only ostracism, but even suspension. (According to a recent "McNeil-Lehrer News Hour" report, one student was suspended for discussing the reality of the moral law with an avowed homosexual. He was reinstated only after he apologized.)

ISBN 1-56384-026-X Trade Paper $9.99

Beyond Political Correctness:
Are There Limits to This Lunacy?
by David Thibodaux

Author of the best-selling *Political Correctness: The Cloning of the American Mind,* Dr. David Thibodaux now presents his long awaited sequel—*Beyond Political Correctness: Are There Limits to This Lunacy?* The politically correct movement has now moved beyond college campuses. The movement has succeeded in turning the educational system of this country into a system of indoctrination. Its effect on education was predictable: steadily declining scores on every conceivable test which measures student performance; and, increasing numbers of college freshmen who know a great deal about condoms, homosexuality, and abortion, but whose basic skills in language, math, and science are alarmingly deficient.

ISBN 1-56384-066-9 $9.99

I Shot an Elephant in My Pajamas— The Morrie Ryskind Story
by Morrie Ryskind with John H. M. Roberts

The Morrie Ryskind story is a classic American success story. The son of Russian Jewish immigrants, Ryskind went on to attend Columbia University and achieve legendary fame on Broadway and in Hollywood, win the Pulitzer Prize, and become a noted nationally syndicated columnist. Writing with his legendary theatrical collaborators George S. Kaufman and George and Ira Gershwin, their political satires had an enormous impact on the development of the musical comedy. In Hollywood, many classic films and four of the Marx Brothers' sublime romps also bear the signatory stamp of genius—Morrie Ryskind. Forced by his increasingly conservative views to abandon script-writing in Hollywood, Ryskind had the satisfaction near the end of his life to welcome into his home his old friend, the newly elected President of the United States, Ronald Reagan.

ISBN 1-56384-000-6 $12.99

The Media Hates Conservatives: How It Controls the Flow of Information
by Dale A. Berryhill

Here is clear and powerful evidence that the liberal leaning news media brazenly attempted to influence the outcome of the election between President George Bush and Candidate Bill Clinton. Through a careful analysis of television and newspaper coverage, this book confirms a consistent pattern of liberal bias (even to the point of assisting the Clinton campaign). The major media outlets have taken sides in the culture war. Through bias, distortion, and the violation of professional standards, they have opposed the traditional values embraced by conservatives and most Americans, to the detriment of our country.

ISBN 1-56384-060-X $9.99

Kinsey, Sex and Fraud:
The Indoctrination of a People
by Dr. Judith A. Reisman and Edward Eichel

Kinsey, Sex and Fraud describes the research of Alfred Kinsey which shaped Western society's beliefs and understanding of the nature of human sexuality. His unchallenged conclusions are taught at every level of education—elementary, high school, and college—and quoted in textbooks as undisputed truth. The authors clearly demonstrate that Kinsey's research involved illegal experimentations on several hundred children. The survey was carried out on a non-representative group of Americans, including disproportionately large numbers of sex offenders, prostitutes, prison inmates, and exhibitionists.

ISBN 0-910311-20-X $10.99

A Jewish Conservative
Looks at Pagan America
by Don Feder

With eloquence and insight that rival essayists of antiquity, Don Feder's pen finds his targets in the enemies of God, family, and American tradition and morality. Deftly . . . delightfully . . . the master allegorist and Titian with a typewriter brings clarity to the most complex sociological issues and invokes giggles and wry smiles from both followers and foes. Feder is Jewish to the core, and he finds in his Judaism no inconsistency with an American Judeo-Christian ethic. Questions of morality plague school administrators, district court judges, senators, congressmen, parents, and employers; they are wrestling for answers in a "changing world." Feder challenges this generation and directs inquirers to the original books of wisdom: the Torah and the Bible.

ISBN 1-56384-036-7 Trade Paper $9.99
ISBN 1-56384-037-5 Hardcover $19.99

Trojan Horse—
How the New Age Movement Infiltrates the Church
by Samantha Smith &
Brenda Scott

New Age/Occult concepts and techniques are being introduced into all major denominations. The revolution is subtle, cumulative, and deadly. Through what door has this heresy entered the church? Authors Samantha Smith and Brenda Scott attempt to demonstrate that Madeleine L'Engle has been and continues to be a major New Age source of entry into the church. Because of her radical departure from traditional Christian theology, Madeleine L'Engle's writings have sparked a wave of controversy across the nation. She has been published and promoted by numerous magazines, including Today's Christian Woman, Christianity Today and others. The deception, unfortunately, has been so successful that otherwise discerning congregations and pastors have fallen into the snare that has been laid.

ISBN 1-56384-040-5 $9.99

High on Adventure
Stories of Good, Clean, Spine-tingling Fun
by Stephen Arrington

From meeting a seventeen-and-a-half-foot great white shark face to face, to diving from an airplane toward the earth's surface at 140 M.P.H., to exploring a sunken battle cruiser from World War II in the dark depths of the South Pacific Ocean, author and adventurer Stephen Arrington retells many exciting tales from his life as a navy frogman and chief diver for the Cousteau Society. Each story is laced with Arrington's Christian belief and outlook that life is an adventure waiting to be had.

ISBN 1-56384-082-0 $7.99

ORDER THESE HUNTINGTON HOUSE BOOKS !

*Available in Salt Series

Available at bookstores everywhere or order direct from:
Huntington House Publishers • P.O. Box 53788 • Lafayette, LA 70505
Send check/money order. For faster service use VISA/MASTERCARD.
Call toll-free 1-800-749-4009.
Add: Freight and handling, $3.50 for the first book ordered, and $.50 for
each additional book up to 5 books.